THE HEART-CENTERED
LEADERSHIP PLAYBOOK

EARLY PRAISE QUOTES FOR: THE HEART-CENTERED LEADERSHIP PLAYBOOK

"*The Heart-Centered Leadership Playbook* is exceptionally perceptive and brimming with excellent observations. A must read for management"

—GARY HENDERSON,
CO-FOUNDER AND CHAIRMAN
LBI PUBLISHING, INC.

"It comes as no surprise to me that Deb writes as she speaks: Eloquently, passionately, directly... and straight from the heart. In every industry and sector, in every country and jurisdiction, there is a dearth of effective leadership. In my world of healthcare, leadership has been conflated with management. People, whether they are those we serve or those that provide the care, are lost in the math. Leadership isn't about X's and O's. Paul Batalden once posed the question to me, "What is the one characteristic of every effective leader?" The answer is that people follow them. Leadership is defined by an outcome: followership. Deb challenges us to become better leaders by leveraging that very human characteristic that compels others to follow: Heart-Centeredness. Such qualities as compassion, kindness, empathy, and vulnerability that emerge from that core piece are what create the connection that make others want to follow. And importantly, TRUST to follow. My hope is that this book will compel a critical mass of leaders, and importantly those about to emerge, to eschew mere wooden leadership recipes and embrace heart-centeredness as an essential piece of how they lead."

—DR. PAUL WOODS, MD, MS

"*The Heart-Centered Leadership Playbook* is creative and bold. It's something that is much needed now. If you genuinely want to create and nurture a wonderful place to work, then you want to be a heart-centered leader."

—GLENN PARKER,

TEAMBUILDING AND LEADERSHIP CONSULTANT

"Deb Crowe has written the ultimate guide in *The Heart-Centered Leadership Playbook* for leaders to transform their approach and boost productivity, improve communication and increase performance and collaboration within their organizations. With profound wisdom and practical insights from her own experience, Deb dives deep into the power of leading from the heart – emphasizing empathy, authenticity, and purpose-driven leadership. This content-rich book offers a refreshing perspective on how compassionate and emotionally intelligent leaders can ignite a sense of purpose, inspire innovation, and unleash the full potential of individuals and teams in their companies. Filled with compelling life stories and practical strategies, along with insights from a variety of exceptional leaders, the book equips readers with the tools they need to cultivate a heart-centered culture of trust, motivation, and productivity. This is a must-read for individuals who seek to make an impact in their companies and in the world through heart-centered leadership."

—DR. LORI BAKER-SCHENA, MBA, EDD

"Most discussions, published works, lectures, mentoring and coaching session about leadership development focus on behaviours (actions) and mention cognitions (perceptions, attitudes, beliefs). Leaders certainly must understand and learn to control behaviours and cognitions, but they also must understand motivations and emotions to optimize leadership. Deb Crowe's Heart-Centered Leadership Playbook clearly focuses on and embraces motivation and emotions in addition to behaviours and cognitions relevant to effective leadership. Her clear prose and story-telling style bring life to the meaningful lessons that she encourages readers to learn. This volume provides a valuable addition and crucial component to the leadership literature."

—NEIL E. GRUNBERG, PH.D.,

MEDICAL PSYCHOLOGIST

AND BEHAVIOURAL NEUROSCIENTIST,

BETHESDA, MARYLAND, USA

"Leadership is not merely about steering a team; it's about guiding hearts. In The Heart-Centered Leadership Playbook, empathy is the strategy, authenticity is the tactic and love is the game-changer."

—LOVEDEEP SINGH

"In *The Heart-Centered Leadership Playbook*, you are sharing your beautifully imperfect heart with the world, and we need you and your expertise - now more than ever. Thank you for being a true beacon of leadership - you are the light that guides our hearts through stormy weather. I have learned from you that my imperfections and non-traditional approaches to leadership are my greatest gifts. Thanks to you, I fearlessly lead with the entire ocean of my heart."

—DANA SCIUTO,

SENIOR WORKPLACE STRATEGIST,

BGIS, ED.D

"In *The Heart-Centered Leadership Playbook* it allowed us as the reader to tap into all of Deborah's knowledge and experience. If this is a glimpse of what you know and offer, please keep writing and sharing!"

—RADA MEDIC,

SENIOR ADVISOR, ESG - LARGE SEGMENT

"Deborah beautifully brought us on a synopsis of your journey to Heart-Centered Leadership. Not only did she share why it matters so much to you, but why it should to the rest of the world. Your vulnerability is admired, and you have inspired me. I will truly inspire others to be more vulnerable within their journey as well."

—MICHAEL WEAVER JR.,

ASSOCIATE DIRECTOR, DONOR & EXTERNAL RELATIONS,

UNIVERSITY OF TEXAS-AUSTIN

THE HEART-CENTERED LEADERSHIP PLAYBOOK:

How to Master the Art of Heart in Life and Leadership

DEBORAH CROWE

MANUSCRIPTS PRESS

THE HEART-CENTERED LEADERSHIP PLAYBOOK:
How to Master the Art of Heart in Life and Leadership

ISBN

979-8-88926-744-7   *Paperback*

979-8-88926-745-4   *Ebook*

To all the courageous souls who dare to lead with their hearts:

This playbook is dedicated to you. You, who possess the unwavering belief in the power of love, compassion, and empathy as catalysts for change. You, who understand that true leadership transcends titles and authority, flowing from the depths of your being into every interaction, every decision, and every vision you bring to life.

To the leaders who choose vulnerability over invulnerability, authenticity over masks, and connection over distance: this is for you. You have embraced the profound truth that the greatest strength lies in showing up fully, embracing your imperfections, and inspiring others to do the same.

In a world often driven by profit margins and competition, you have chosen a different path—a path guided by values, purpose, and the genuine desire to create a positive impact. You have recognized that success is not solely measured by financial gain, but by the lives touched, the souls uplifted, and the love shared along the way.

This playbook seeks to honor your commitment by offering guidance, insights, and practical wisdom that align with the beat of your compassionate heart. It is a heartfelt reminder that true leadership stems from a place of deep inner knowing, of staying attuned to the whispers of intuition, and of honoring the sacredness of each human connection you forge.

May these pages serve as a compass, illuminating the path to heart-centered leadership—a path that intertwines empathy with strategy, mindfulness with action, and love with accountability. May it inspire you to lead not only with your mind but also with your heart, recognizing that the greatest transformations occur when passion is infused with compassion.

To the leaders who are daring enough to dream big, to reimagine possibilities, and to embody a vision that celebrates the collective well-being of all: this playbook is a humble offering. May it provide you with the tools and inspiration to navigate the challenges, embrace the joys, and cultivate the immense potential that lies within you and within every person you lead.

With deepest admiration and gratitude,

DEBORAH CROWE

FOREWORD

---

by Hugh MacLeod

Greetings,

As a fellow author and lifelong learner, I feel incredibly privileged to have the opportunity to write the foreword for this remarkable book. Throughout my journey as a front-line worker, middle manager, senior executive, senior government bureaucrat, and chief operating officer, I've gained a profound appreciation for the intricate dynamics that unfold within and between organizational spaces.

In 2019, I had the pleasure of publishing my own book, *Humanizing Leadership*. It was during this time that I had the good fortune of connecting with Deb. From our very first Zoom chat, an instant connection was forged, and our relationship has continued to flourish ever since. When I reflect upon why our connection is so strong, the answer is clear: we both share a passion for elevating the human element of relationships. Through our shared experiences, we demonstrate an openness of mind, heart, and will.

Our first heart-centered conversation was a profound experience, sparked by a personal insight I shared with Deb. I expressed how being drawn to leadership is tantamount to being drawn to the heart of human conditions, and how I often found myself held captive by misplaced ego, the façade of omniscience, avoidance of vulnerability and limitations, and a failure to tap into the brilliance of those around me.

Over the past three and a half years, I've witnessed firsthand how Deb's personal and professional way of being is firmly rooted in "heart-centered leadership." What you see and read is an authentic representation of who she truly is. Heart-centered leadership is the cornerstone of her consistency, her guiding principles, and her personal mission and legacy.

In books of this nature, it is crucial to feel a genuine connection with the author, finding them wise, likable, or both. In Deb's case, she embodies both. Unlike other authors who lead with their own expertise, Deb leads with humility, sharing her own vulnerabilities and recognizing that both she and the reader have much to learn from one another.

In these unprecedented times, this is the book that all leaders should read and share with their teams. It provides invaluable insights on how to pivot and serve both people and culture simultaneously. Deb's candid approach, devoid of ambiguous language or attempts to conceal the truth, is powerful. Collectively, the contents of this book make a compelling case that personal learning and growth are not merely about what you have done or achieved, but about what you choose to do next.

The "Full-Circle Moments" that conclude each chapter are a brilliant addition. They offer clear takeaways about both internal and external relationships. This book is not an academic lecture; rather, it is a genuine conversation with the reader.

Our innate human reflex often leads us to automatically judge the world as separate and distinct from ourselves. However, with heart-centered leadership, the journey begins with a relationship between one and oneself. By cultivating this foundational inner relationship, one can authentically extend it outward to others and establish meaningful, balanced connections.

Deb's leadership experiences across multiple sectors and continents have shaped her heart-centered approach into something both eloquent and inviting. She challenges us on our personal and professional journey of discovery, urging us to shift our focus from the outside in to the inside out. Operating from the "inside out" entails observing the internal states that drive our responses to the external world.

In this book, Deb reminds us that organizational culture is a tapestry woven from interconnected circles of complex human activity, patterns of energy, and webs of relationships, conversations, and decisions.

The personal stories shared here serve as seeds planted by a compassionate and caring gardener, and indeed the metaphor of gardening beautifully encapsulates the essence of this book. The alignment of intention between gardeners and heart-centered leaders is remarkable.

Gardeners understand that cultivation requires time, attention, nurturing, protection, patience, understanding, and preparedness for environmental challenges. Heart-centered leaders align themselves with the gardener's perspective, recognizing that their people are the garden. Patience, kindness, time, and space for growth are vital to their success too. Each person is unique, and there is no one-size-fits-all system or template. Regular check-ins and alignment of life and work (the watering) are essential for sustaining continuous growth.

Planting a seed does not guarantee growth. It is essential to have intentions without expecting reciprocity. A heart-centered gardener tends to both what is visible above the surface and what is hidden below.

Have you taken the time to reevaluate and adjust your leadership blueprint as necessary? Are your expectations aligned with everyone's individual growth patterns? Have you provided optimal conditions for growth? Do you accept that development is not always a linear process? Do you communicate in a manner that captivates others' attention, and do you listen in a way that encourages others to share? Have you embraced the hands-on responsibility of your leadership?

Welcome to *The Heart-Centered Leadership Playbook*, a personal journey of discovery that will expand your mind, open your heart, and strengthen your will. With intention, from the inside out, this book will connect your values and passions, allowing you to lead with purpose and create a lasting impact.

—HUGH MACLEOD, ADJUNCT PROFESSOR,
AUTHOR, AND FRIEND OF DEBORAH

CONTENTS

———

A MANIFESTO FOR THE HEART-CENTERED LEADER

―――

As a heart-centered leader, I believe in:

1. The power of compassion and connection to create a better world.
2. Leading with an open heart and creating an inclusive and equitable environment.
3. Striving to create a space where everyone is respected, heard, and valued.
4. The importance of collaboration and innovation.
5. Prioritizing listening to the voices of my team.
6. Creating a safe space for dialogue and creative problem-solving.
7. Fostering an environment of mutual respect, understanding, and trust.
8. Recognizing the power of empathy in building solid relationships and learning.

9. Leading with kindness and creating an inclusive environment for all.
10. Modeling the importance of self-care and balance to lead with a whole heart.
11. Understanding that leading with an open heart is a lifelong journey.
12. Staying humble and open-minded, to be willing to learn and grow.
13. As a heart-centered leader, I am committed to creating a better world for all.

The heart has its own language.
The heart knows a hundred thousand ways to speak.

—RUMI

♥

Your vision will become clear only
when you look into your heart.

Who looks outside, dreams,
who looks inside, awakens.

—CARL JUNG

♥

INTRODUCTION

Leadership isn't about giving orders and making decisions. It's about inspiring others to greatness and creating a world that works for everyone.

Heart-centered leadership is the key to unlocking the full potential of your team and yourself. In this book, you'll discover the secrets to leading with empathy, compassion, and authenticity, and how to create a culture of trust and collaboration that empowers everyone to succeed. Get ready to transform your leadership and change the world, one heart at a time.

Too many leadership models lead to suffering, alienation, missed opportunities, and poorer results. The existing leadership playbooks are full of extrinsic and systematic processes. They're missing the "heart."

Heart-centered leadership is honoring your connection with people. There's no agenda or room for transactional dynamics.

A heart-centered leadership approach brings tremendous value to organizations, teams, and individuals.

Here are some of the key benefits:

- Increased engagement and motivation: When leaders lead with empathy and compassion, they create a work environment where people feel valued, heard, and appreciated. This, in turn, leads to higher levels of drive among team members.
- Improved communication and collaboration: Heart-centered leaders prioritize effective interfacing and cooperation, creating an environment where people feel comfortable sharing ideas and working together toward a common goal.
- Enhanced creativity and innovation: When people feel safe and supported, they are more likely to take risks and think outside the box.
- Increased productivity and performance: Heart-centered leaders recognize the importance of work-life balance and invest in the well-being of their team members to prevent burnout and boost operations.
- Greater impact and fulfillment: Heart-centered leaders focus on creating a positive impact in the world, whether through their organization's mission or their individual contributions. This leads to a sense of purpose and accomplishment that goes beyond traditional measures of success.

A heart-centered leadership approach creates a more positive, collaborative, and productive work environment that benefits everyone involved.

In writing this book for leaders, I am seeking to revolutionize their leadership approach, enhance productivity, foster effective communication, and elevate performance and collaboration within themselves and their organization. I've drawn from my own extensive experience to do so.

We will delve into the transformative power of leading with empathy, authenticity, and purpose. Through my practical wisdom, these pages present a fresh perspective on how compassionate and emotionally intelligent leaders can ignite a shared sense of purpose, inspire innovation, and unleash the full potential of individuals and teams within their companies.

Enriched with captivating life stories, actionable strategies, and wisdom from exceptional leaders, this book equips readers with the necessary tools to cultivate a heart-centered culture of trust, motivation, and productivity. It is an indispensable read for those who aspire to make a meaningful impact through heart-centered leadership, both within their organizations and in the wider world.

I have embraced this leadership approach because business acumen is structured to be serious and focused on process, measurement, and financial outcomes. But these components cannot be driven or measured without the human element at the helm. People brave enough to be themselves, speak their minds, and lead from the inside out—with heart—are the champions. They know their connection with people is the key ingredient to the overall success of their organization.

When we allow our grace and imperfection to show up, our lives shine with authenticity, vulnerability, and genuine human connection. It's a self-audit that I have coined

"Mindset Reset," which allows for the rejuvenation of your mind, body, and soul.

When we can decide that we no longer must do anything in obligation, we can be open-minded and self-directed in everything we choose to do and be. The best part is that we'll land within a serendipitous moment of being exactly where we should be.

Leaders who want to bring humanity back into leadership must learn to see beyond the rigid confines of the organizational chart and find significance in the voids between departments and divisions.

When I look around at the current climate of the business world, I witness very few leaders who have the emotional intelligence, cross-cultural relationship-building skills, openness of mind and heart, and the will needed for heart-centered leadership.

Leaders with self-awareness know this truth lies within their inner world. They also know it's difficult to implement and takes time and patience because, today, heart-centered leadership does not exist in language or action within standard business acumen. Developing these qualities takes a lifelong dedication to learning and self-improvement, which currently are not valued in transactional leadership cultures.

Still, I want to be clear that there are many heart-centered leaders around the globe. I have the honor and privilege of working with them daily. Some companies do lead with heart and have genuine, healthy, vital cultures—companies that have written heart-centered language in their constitution. When companies can behave (action) their brand, that, to me, is pure alignment.

This playbook is for anyone who believes they are a leader. We all can continue to learn from each other, evolve, and not have our value system, or worth and worthiness, attached to an identity—especially a job title and the responsibilities that come with it.

This book is for everyone because we are all leaders. When we can bring all that we are to all that we do with humility, transparency, and vulnerability—that is heart-centered leadership.

You don't need initials after your name to be kind.

♥

A brave leader is someone who
says I see you. I hear you.

I don't have all the answers,
but I'm going to keep listening
and asking questions.

—BRENÉ BROWN

♥

CHAPTER 1

EMBRACING THE CALL TO LEADERSHIP

In the vast expanse where leaders are forged and dreams take flight, what are the core qualities that define exceptional leadership? And how can we cultivate these qualities within ourselves to inspire, guide, and empower others on the path to success?

The landscape of heart-centered leadership is more than stature, titles, fancy corner offices, and business suits. It is a terrain that provides us with a journey to the unknown—to the depths of our inner being and to limitless self-awareness.

EMBRACING THE CALL

Embracing leadership and finding joy in the journey can be a transformative and fulfilling experience.

When I reminisce about my own life and leadership experiences, I can clearly define elements that have helped me. I also use these strategies to help my leadership clients globally.

To help you cultivate these qualities in yourself, here's a list of ten strategies.

14. Clarify your vision: Take the time to define your personal and professional image. What do you want to achieve as a leader? What values do you want to embody? Having a clearly defined vision will guide your actions and provide a sense of purpose.

15. Develop self-awareness: Understanding your strengths, weaknesses, and values is crucial for effective leadership. Reflect on your abilities, personality traits, and areas for growth. Seek feedback from others to gain different perspectives. This self-awareness will enable you to lead authentically.

16. Cultivate a growth mindset: Embrace the belief that you can continually learn and improve as a leader. Emphasize growth and development over fixed abilities. Embrace challenges as opportunities for growth and see setbacks as valuable lessons.

17. Lead with empathy: Effective leadership involves understanding and connecting with others. Develop empathy by actively listening, seeking to understand different perspectives, and demonstrating compassion. This will foster trust, collaboration, and a positive work environment.

18. Communicate effectively: Clear and open communication is essential for successful leadership. Practice active listening, articulate your thoughts clearly, and

encourage open dialogue within your team. Provide feedback constructively and recognize the achievements of others.

19. Delegate and empower others: As a leader, you do not have to do everything yourself. Delegate tasks and responsibilities to others, empowering them to take ownership and grow. Trust in their abilities and provide support when needed.

20. Embrace resilience: Leadership journeys often involve challenges and obstacles. Cultivate strength by maintaining a positive mindset, staying adaptable, and focusing on solutions rather than dwelling on problems. Welcome failure as a steppingstone toward success.

21. Foster a learning culture: Encourage continuous learning and growth within your team. Support professional development opportunities, provide mentorship, and foster a culture of curiosity and innovation.

22. Celebrate progress and milestones: Acknowledge and celebrate individual and team achievements. Recognize the progress made toward goals, both big and small. Celebrating milestones boosts morale, creates a positive atmosphere, and reinforces a sense of joy and fulfillment.

23. Practice self-care: Leadership can be demanding, so taking care of yourself is crucial. Prioritize self-care activities like exercise, rest, and hobbies. Maintain a healthy work-life integration to avoid burnout and sustain your enthusiasm.

Remember, leadership is a continuous journey of growth and learning. Embrace the challenges, celebrate successes, and enjoy becoming a better leader.

REVIEWING THE LEADERSHIP JOURNEY

The only time we have is now. I am still learning, growing, and evolving as a woman and a heart-centered leader. There is no destination. The moment we all realize this reality and align our hearts and mind, we start the journey of our lifetime, which is full of joy and truly anchored in the present moment.

I knew from a young age who I was. I could feel things viscerally but could not interpret or express my emotions. Our wisdom increases tenfold through lived experience and education. In that unclear and early life stage, I discovered that leaning into discomfort can be magical, innovative, and provide clarity.

Those moments in life that take our breath away and make our heart pump so hard we think it'll burst out of our chest: That is this book's level of energy, love, and compassion.

I chose to write from a deep space within my heart, a place I call the uncharted sea and beyond the ordinary.

I have been leading uniquely for most of my life—call it survival, instinct, or heart-centered—and now the world is joining in.

While writing this book, I looked deep inside myself. After experiencing traumatic events and loss, my head and heart needed to realign, and I was unsure what was next. Being a volunteer has provided me with a sense of community since the age of twelve, so I turned in that direction.

This is why I chose to become a hospice volunteer: to help me navigate my own grief. Because I have often been alone in challenging times, with little or no support, I developed a wall of resistance to buttress my emotional resilience. Hospice became a haven, a home for me—a place to heal and help simultaneously.

Being among beautiful people and their families at the end of life was a gift that comforted me every week. What was hard for so many was easy for me. As a caregiver, I smoothly navigated the grief road; I knew the level and cycles of emotions that people experience.

This volunteer position gave me time in a unique way. Always in the moment, I embraced my ability to be an attentive listener and spend time with whoever needed me. It was a powerful gift—an heirloom memory engraved in my heart to this day.

Little did I know I would reunite with my father's cardiologist, my high-school friend's mother, a friend from a previous workplace, and many other notable people along the way. It renewed my faith that I *am* a leader on many levels and that being heart-centered is truly a gift.

LEADERSHIP: A JOURNEY OF BEING AND BECOMING

I have lived in a heart-centered world my whole life. I have seen the best and the worst that people and life can hand us. I have also experienced profound loss and trauma, both personally and professionally. But I decided not to wallow in these experiences; I became someone with a prominent level of emotional intelligence and a solid foundation of emotional resilience.

I am an introvert who spends much time in deep thought—so I decided to take these life experiences, make them learning moments, and added them to my ever-growing heart-centered leadership toolkit. The joy and power in perspective are significant.

Having lived a heart-centered life, I have been told I am too loving and giving and do too much for others. And believe me—various leaders did not share these comments with me in a positive spirit. If that is how I am described, I will continue to have influence, even if the world has yet to adapt to this kind of playbook.

Of course, there are other leadership playbooks in the world today. But I have been looking for one that reflects heart-centered leadership.

I couldn't find it, so I wrote one.

Let's break down my theory and practical application of a heart-centered leadership playbook:

Heart-centered leadership is honoring our connection with people. Playbook, from the Cambridge Dictionary, means "the person or people in charge of an organization." When we combine the descriptions, the resulting playbook will help you gain the knowledge and tools to honor your connection with people in life and leadership.

NAVIGATING LEADERSHIP IN A BURDENED WORLD

The world is heavy.

Recently, the global pandemic changed how we look at life and the world. We had time to pause. We had time to think and review all aspects of our lives. We had time to see, feel, and value everything and everyone around us.

The pandemic opened a new level of human kindness—after all, we were at home for two years, missing human interaction and connection. Compounding that were the fast pace of technology and overall changes that came with not being physically connected.

The best success is not measured by a raise in pay, a pat on the back, or a new office. While those are extrinsically lovely moments in our lives, they are not heartfelt or connected to our inner being.

Being imperfect, laughed at, bullied, not included, feeling like an outlier, and taken advantage of—these are the challenges that have shaped me. These moments are the foundation and depth of my heart-centered leadership.

They reinforced a value my Irish Nana instilled in me at the tender age of eight: Kindness will never go out of style. I can always control how I feel and, more importantly, how I respond.

This is something I work at daily, and it has taken me years to reach this level of self-awareness and equanimity.

After thirty-three years in business, I am receiving all the goodness in my life. The whispers in my mind, remarkably silent on some days, always eventually showed up to say, "Keep going—you're doing it the right way." That was the fuel I needed and longed to hear. It came from my inner voice. I know now deep in my heart that I put something in motion from my first day in kindergarten, when I sensed that something grander was coming to me someday. I stayed in that mindset and knew I would be ready when it was time.

FULL-CIRCLE LIFE MOMENT:

My superpower is making a difference by continuing to be a heart-centered leader. I would love for you to join me, and as global citizens, we can make a ripple effect of goodness in our world.

♥

You have to keep breaking
your heart until it opens.

—RUMI

♥

CHAPTER 2

KINDNESS IS THE WAY

What if the most powerful tool in a leader's arsenal is not their position or authority, but their kindness?

What if I asked you to leave space to *un*lead—to go on a leadership journey of discovery back to your birth, then to your first day of kindergarten, elementary school, high school, trade school, undergrad, post-grad, and every job you've had—and then you created a space to see what intrinsic and extrinsic motivators brought you to where you are today as a leader?

It was Sunday, September 13, 1987—a typical fall morning. I could hear my mother screaming from upstairs; I was in my bedroom, sound asleep in the basement. As a post-secondary student, I loved sleeping in on the weekend. As I heard my mother continuing to scream, I thought I was dreaming. When the screaming only went on and got louder, I partially awoke, disoriented; my first reaction was that I was late for school. When I woke up and ran up the stairs, the look on my mother's face said it all.

She said, "Get dressed; we must go to the hospital. Your father has just passed away."

It was half past six in the morning, and I was twenty-one years old. I fell to my knees on the stairs with tears streaming down my face. I was frozen. I couldn't process what had been said to me. There was no hug, conversation, nothing. That moment was the day I knew I was going to grow up quickly. That was the start of my leadership journey, and the day I realized emotional resilience would be in my toolkit for the rest of my life.

My last conversation with my dad was the evening before, and we both knew it was the end of his life. That night, he said two things to me that have been engraved in my heart and are foundational to my growth as a woman, daughter, wife, mother, and leader.

He said:

"It would help if you found a way to work with people."

and

"Don't ever say you don't know. We all have a working knowledge of everything. Adapt, push yourself and learn."

How is that for emotional resilience training?

I am an outlier. I have always felt like I didn't belong wherever I lived or was. I am a leader. I am the round peg in the square hole. I own it, love it, and lead with who I am and with heart.

For most of my childhood and developmental years, I had a corneal ulcer in my right eye—and going through life with one eye behind a patch forced my brain to think differently.

Your brain can teach itself a new set of things too. Welcome to the new neuropathways!

Heart-centered people have many conversations with themselves. It's a deep level of self-awareness. All problems can be solved from the heart. My Irish Nana used to say to me, "Do the best you can with the tools you have. We don't have to build a parachute on the way down."

Leadership is not one specific element. And each leader brings their uniqueness to the role. It's not their title or responsibilities that make them a great leader; it's the sum of their life, work, and academic experience.

Every day we have the option to choose fear over joy—because fear will always leave joy behind. When we live in hope, it gives us the present of living in the moment.

If we allow doubt to enter our thoughts, it feeds skepticism and limits us to having no regulation over our emotions. When we get stuck in this thinking pattern, it's hard to transition. To progress into being unstuck, choosing hope over doubt is our best modality.

Can you rest with comfort and ease in the present moment? When I reflect on learning how to be in the "now," I immediately think of a pivotal, emotional memory.

It was International Women's Day 2019. I was sitting at a prestigious private club attending a function and I was also a speaker at this event. As I listened to the keynote speaker and learned about tall poppy syndrome my heart started beating like it was going to fall out of my chest.

What is tall poppy syndrome?

Tall poppy syndrome, a term made popular in Australia, refers to the phenomenon where individuals face attacks, resentment, dislike, criticism, or being cut down solely because of their achievements and success. This silent systemic syndrome has significant consequences, particularly on women in the workplace. This new knowledge struck a chord: I experienced prolonged tall poppy syndrome when I returned to work after my dad passed away. Those were three of the most challenging years of my life—all spent working with unkind women.

My dad instilled in me that I should always be early to work. Keep my desk organized. Be a team player and don't rush out the door at five or be a clock watcher.

I prided myself on being kind, friendly, smiling, and collaborating. But then, I would get to the review at the end of the probation period only to hear that I was:

- Too happy
- Too gregarious
- Too smiley
- Too loud
- Laughed too much

- Too chatty
- "A lot"

As I sat in that venue all those years later in 2020, tears started streaming down my face. Back then, I had been criticized for being kind-hearted, hard-working, and friendly—and now I was having a serious realization about the fallout.

For thirty-three years, I internalized that it was *me*. That there was something wrong with me.

I can remember the first women leader that did this. But as I reflect now, I realize that her unkindness was about her own life—being mid-fifties, overweight, unhappy, divorced— and not mine.

From there, I moved to my next job: administrative assistant in a very successful real estate firm. When I received a brand-new typewriter and looked at the manual, I realized it had memory built in! My visionary brain immediately thought of all the repetitive clauses in a real estate offer. I proceeded to teach myself how to input all the most common clauses—and the next thing I had was a lineup of real estate agents at my desk.

Still, when my probation date approached, the manager looked at me and said, "It's just not working."

I wanted to collapse on the floor—I had been working so hard for three months! The high-producing agents could not believe I was being let go. But I didn't fit in. The world was moving me on. Again.

I tried to figure out what the lesson was. Why was I not hired?

That's when I began delving into the realm of cognitive thinking, which subsequently opened numerous new opportunities for me. This realization highlights the fact that sometimes we are nudged toward different paths, and not all these experiences may be positive.

I started to think about how I felt and my thinking habits at this stage in life.

This was my first exploration of "metacognition"—a neuroscience term defined as how we think about thinking. I have always thought and acted from a place of kindness. This has been variably embraced, used, and abused—but I always fell back into gratitude. I know who I am, and compassion will never go out of style.

On May 30, 1990, I started my own company. I was twenty-four and soaring on great advice from a heart-centered VP at the last company that let me go: the world needs your type of leadership, so go out on your own and lead.

Being a kind leader is an admirable goal that can positively impact your team and create a supportive work environment. Let's look at how you think about thinking when it comes to your leadership and kindness.

Here are some heart-centered strategies on how to be a kind leader.

1. Show empathy: Take the time to understand and acknowledge your team members' feelings and perspectives. Really listen to them and be genuinely interested in their well-being.
2. Lead by example: Demonstrate kindness in your actions and interactions. Treat others with respect and fairness. Your behavior sets the tone for the team, so strive to be a role model.
3. Communicate effectively: Clearly and openly communicate with your team members. Be transparent about expectations, goals, and feedback. Use constructive criticism and focus on providing guidance and support rather than belittling or criticizing.
4. Foster a supportive environment: Encourage collaboration and teamwork by creating an atmosphere of trust and psychological safety. Encourage open communication, idea sharing, and respect for diverse opinions.
5. Practice active appreciation: Regularly acknowledge and appreciate everyone's efforts and achievements. Recognize their hard work, celebrate successes, and publicly express gratitude for their contributions. This helps boost morale and creates a positive work culture.
6. Provide opportunities for growth: Support your team's professional development by providing them with learning opportunities, training, and challenges that help them grow and achieve their career goals. Show genuine interest in their development and provide guidance and mentorship when needed.
7. Be approachable and accessible: Create an open-door policy where your team feels comfortable coming to

you with questions, concerns, or suggestions. Be available to listen and provide guidance when needed.

8. Practice conflict resolution: Kind leadership involves handling conflicts in a respectful and constructive manner. Encourage open communication and address conflicts promptly and fairly. Focus on finding solutions that benefit everyone involved.

9. Take care of yourself: As a leader, it's important to take care of your own well-being. Prioritize self-care and stress management, as this will only enhance your ability to lead with kindness and empathy.

Remember, being a kind leader is an ongoing process. It requires consistent effort, self-reflection, and a genuine desire to support and uplift others.

FULL-CIRCLE LIFE MOMENT:
A bright light is not for everyone—but that doesn't mean you can't keep moving forward and shining brighter.

♥

People don't care
how much you know
until they know
how much you care.

—JOHN C. MAXWELL

♥

CHAPTER 3

THE HEART-CENTERED LEADERSHIP BILL OF RIGHTS

———

What if we could create a world where every individual's well-being and empowerment were a top priority in the workplace?

What if we could establish a Heart-Centered Leadership Bill of Rights that guaranteed every person the right to be seen, heard, and valued by all leaders in their organization?

Let's explore these questions and more as we dive further into the transformative power of heart-centered leadership.

Every person deserves to be led by someone who values their humanity—who sees them not only as an employee, but as a whole person with thoughts, feelings, and aspirations.

Outlined below are the fundamental principles of leadership that prioritize the well-being and empowerment of every individual. Learn how to embrace these principles and create a work environment where everyone feels valued, respected, and heard. It's time to take a stand for heart-centered leadership and create a better world for ourselves and future generations.

A bill of rights, also known as a declaration of rights or charter of rights, is a list of principles that are considered to be fundamental to those under its purview.

Review this Bill of Rights and see how it can serve you in both your daily life and leadership:

You have the right to never feel bad about saying no (or yes) to others. Boundary management is key for all, whether we are at work or living our own lives.

You have the right to deviate from the intended path or to alter your mind. When we are being and leading with heart, our own thoughts, feelings, and emotions matter. Having our own opinion is key, as is having a difference of opinions. This opens an opportunity for a meaningful and aligned conversation.

You have the right to obtain your desired outcomes through discussion and compromise. It's easy for us to get stuck and feel a certain way, which is why it's important for us to ensure we have proper boundaries in place.

You have the right to say all that you are feeling. At any moment in time, your words could be life-changing for someone.

You have the right to share your thoughts even if they're not shared by others. Everyone is entitled to their opinion. The best ideas and outcomes come from collaboration and everyone sharing their thoughts.

You have the right to be treated with kindness, thoughtfulness, and respect. Every human being has these basic needs. You have the right to remove yourself from anyone or any situation, and to not be part of an abusive situation.

You have the right to choose who is allowed to share in your life. Proper boundary management allows us the space to spend time with those people who lift us up and encourage us to be better. We have one life; spend your time wisely, as it is your richest commodity. Be with the people who light you up.

You have the right to share your limits and non-negotiables. We all have our physical, cognitive, emotional, and psychological limits. When you have inner clarity, it's easy to share what your belief and value system is and that you choose not to waiver from it.

You have the right to put yourself first without guilt. Self-care does not have to be seen as selfish. When you can implement and model self-care, it truly gifts you the ability to be your best self in all that you do.

You have the right to be yourself, let your true self shine through, and enjoy your life. It is our birthright to be who we are born to be. Shine your light. Let it be bright. You cannot please everyone, but you will live a meaningful life. Following the pack or trend isn't always the way. Intentionally carving out your own path is courageous and admirable.

Implementing this Bill of Rights is the fun part!

How, why, or when are these rights integrated into leadership?

Let's start with the "how?" Leaders from all sectors ask me this question daily. The first step in learning how to integrate these rights is to complete a self-audit to ensure you fully understand each one and how they can be manifested into your daily leadership skills. Once you understand and practice, the beauty is sharing this with others.

Why would we want to implement these rights?

Every person longs to be seen, heard, and validated. When we are in someone's presence, we have the choice to be fully present with them. Our presence is wholehearted when we are there for no other reason than respect. There is no agenda and no room for any transactional value or non-reciprocity.

When these rights are implemented, they provide a beautiful foundation for your leadership. Whether you want to integrate them into daily living or continue to practice with your co-workers, friends, and team at work—these rights are fundamental. If we are truly heart-centered, our environment really doesn't matter because these rights are demonstrated in our leadership skills as a human being.

You can find the image version of this Heart-Centered Leadership Bill of Rights toward the end of the book in the Resources section.

FULL-CIRCLE LIFE MOMENT:
Knowing when to speak is vital. Knowing when to listen is essential. Never allow anyone to dim your light. Growth comes from discomfort and, sometimes, we must navigate to eventual comfort by first speaking our truth.

♥

Anyone who claims to be a leader
must speak like a leader.

That means speaking with
integrity and truth.

—KAMALA HARRIS

♥

CHAPTER 4

HEART-CENTERED LEADERSHIP AFFIRMATIONS

———

What if you could lead with your heart every day, knowing that your actions were making a positive impact on the world around you?

What if you could embrace the power of compassion, empathy, and authenticity to create a work environment that lifts everyone up?

Let's discover some heart-centered affirmations that will guide you on your journey toward becoming the kind of leader that inspires greatness in others.

Prepare to tap into your inner wisdom and unleash your full potential as a heart-centered leader.

This affirmation list was developed as a tool to help all people at different levels of leadership. Its original goal was to instill in my students the habit of thinking about what they learned from a heart-centered leadership micro-credential series that I developed and teach as a college professor. It's easy to learn something new from a course and then move forward but not implement what we have learned.

HEART-CENTERED LEADERSHIP AFFIRMATIONS:

- I have the ability to lead and inspire others.
- My leadership qualities are evident to everyone around me. Over the years, I have developed the ability to lead a wide variety of people in any circumstance.
- I have a level of natural charisma that people find irresistible. That makes it easy for people to trust and believe in my words and my vision. People are attracted to me and what I have to say. I am a person that people follow willingly.
- It is my ability to inspire others that sets me apart.
- I know how to motivate people and present a possible future that others find attractive. When I inspire others, they can give me their best each day. When I inspire others to do their best, I demonstrate the depth of my leadership skills.
- I am always perfecting my ability to lead and inspire. Though I already know so much, I can always learn more. I avoid becoming lazy and complacent. I am continuously improving my skills.
- Leadership skills are at a premium in today's world. I know that my skills are valued throughout the world.
- As my ability to lead grows, the number of opportunities available to me grows as well.

- Today, I am taking full advantage of any opportunity to lead and inspire others. I am doing my best to be a great leader as I work on strengthening my leadership skills even further.

This list has helped many heart-centered leaders as a daily self-check—to ensure that they are prepared for a meeting, conversation, or presentation.

Affirmations are powerful statements that focus on personal strengths, values, and aspirations. When applied in a heart-centered manner, they emphasize empathy, compassion, and connection.

By incorporating these affirmations into the workplace, individuals and teams can cultivate a sense of self-worth, confidence, and motivation.

Heart-centered affirmations also encourage a shift from competition to collaboration, nurturing a collective mindset that values cooperation, kindness, and understanding.

They promote emotional well-being, reduce stress, and enhance communication, leading to improved relationships and increased productivity.

They help build resilience, enhance self-esteem, and develop a strong sense of our self-worth.

They empower individuals to bring their whole selves to work, creating an inclusive and harmonious workplace where everyone can thrive.

Ultimately, they can be incredibly beneficial for everyone, supporting their emotional well-being and overall growth through a positive framework for self-reflection and self-empowerment.

We are all students in life—still navigating and learning. Imagine if we approached daily learning in this context.

Heart-centered affirmations have the remarkable power to transform your leadership by cultivating a profound connection between your inner self and outward actions. When you engage in them you tap into the wellspring of love, compassion, and authenticity that resides within you. By consciously affirming positive beliefs about yourself and your leadership abilities, you align your thoughts, emotions, and intentions with the core values that guide how you lead.

This alignment fosters a deep sense of self-awareness, empathy, and understanding, enabling you to lead with greater authenticity and compassion. As you consistently practice heart-centered affirmations, they begin to reshape your mindset, rewiring your thoughts and beliefs to be more supportive, empowering, and uplifting.

This transformative process empowers you to inspire and motivate others, foster meaningful connections, and create a positive and inclusive work environment. Ultimately, heart-centered affirmations infuse your leadership with a genuine and heartfelt essence, unlocking your full potential as a leader and enabling you to make a lasting positive impact on those around you.

LEADERSHIP AT ALL LEVELS

When I think back to 1990 when I started my own company at age twenty-four, I was so young. I would have welcomed an affirmation list to help shape, guide, and foster my learning and overall advancement in my own leadership.

I firmly believe we learn from our mistakes and that leaning into imperfection has its place in leadership. My point here is that even though I had no support at the start, I still evolved into a heart-centered leader and learned along the way. It was a bumpy road—yet my passion, tenacity, grit, and love for people accompanied me on this journey of life and aligned beautifully with my leadership development.

Growing in leadership is not limited by age. Regardless of the years lived, there are several ways to foster your leadership skills and continue your personal and professional growth.

Here are some heart-centered strategies that can help anyone, at any life stage, develop and enhance their leadership abilities.

1. Continuous Learning: Embrace a mindset of continuous learning. Look for opportunities to expand your knowledge and skills in areas relevant to leadership, such as communication, decision making, strategic thinking, and emotional intelligence. Attend workshops, seminars, and webinars, and read books or articles on leadership.
2. Seek Feedback: Actively seek feedback from others, including colleagues, mentors, supervisors, and team members. Be open to constructive criticism and use

it as an opportunity to improve your leadership style and effectiveness.

3. Set Clear Goals: Establish clear and measurable goals for your development. Identify specific areas you want to improve then set actionable steps to achieve those goals. Regularly assess your progress and adjust as needed.

4. Embrace Challenges: Seek out challenging situations and projects that stretch your leadership capabilities. Stepping outside of your comfort zone allows you to develop new skills, problem-solving abilities, and resilience.

5. Build Relationships: Cultivate strong relationships with your team members, colleagues, and other professionals in your field. Effective leadership relies on trust and collaboration. Invest time in developing rapport, active listening, and understanding the needs and perspectives of others.

6. Lead by Example: Demonstrate the qualities you expect from others. Be a role model by embodying integrity, accountability, empathy, and professionalism. Inspire and motivate others through your actions and words.

7. Seek Leadership Opportunities: Look for further opportunities to lead within your current organization or community. Take on new responsibilities, volunteer for projects, or start initiatives that showcase your leadership abilities. Even small opportunities can provide valuable experience and help you grow.

8. Build a Support Network: Surround yourself with a supportive network of mentors, coaches, and peers who can provide guidance, advice, and support. Engage in networking activities to connect with like-minded individuals who can share insights and experiences.

9. Reflect and Self-Assess: Regularly reflect on your leadership experiences and evaluate your strengths and areas for improvement. Engage in self-assessment to identify your leadership style, values, and areas where you can enhance your skills. Use tools like journaling or self-reflection exercises to gain deeper insight.
10. Adapt to Change: Leadership requires adaptability in an ever-changing world. Stay abreast of industry trends, technological advancements, and societal shifts. Develop the ability to navigate uncertainty, embrace innovation, and lead through change.

Remember that leadership growth is a continuous process. Embrace opportunities for growth, be open to feedback, and remain committed to developing your skills throughout your life, regardless of your age.

SELF-REFLECTION QUESTIONS:
- What opportunities do I have to become a heart-centered leader in my life?
- What can I do to enhance my leadership abilities?
- What are my greatest strengths as a leader?

FULL-CIRCLE LIFE MOMENT:
It's easy to look back on our lives and be self-critical. But there is magic in learning. Imperfection guides us to learn, grow, do, and be the best version of ourselves. I wouldn't change any season of my life; each has provided lessons, reasoning, and continual growth.

♥

We see the world, not as it is,
but as we are—or, as we are
conditioned to see it.

—STEPHEN R. COVEY

♥

CHAPTER 5

MIDLIFE WISDOM— EMBRACE BEING A MODERN ELDER

What if we viewed midlife not as a crisis—but as an opportunity for growth, transformation, and longevity?

Let's challenge the traditional notion of the midlife crisis and explore the unique potential that comes with this phase of life.

Changing your outlook and uncovering ways to utilize your experience and wisdom to become a more impactful and compassionate heart-centered leader.

The world is changing at an unprecedented pace, and the skills and knowledge that once made us successful may no longer be enough. As a modern elder (forty-five years and older), you have the unique opportunity to bridge the gap between traditional wisdom and modern innovation.

We will explore what it means to be a modern elder: To leverage your experience and insights to become a more effective and compassionate leader. To embrace the power of your wisdom and lead with your heart in a rapidly changing world.

Most people candidly declare that midlife can, and will, be a crisis. But I am an eternal optimist and embrace all midlife wisdom.

I am seven years into my fifties, and it has been transformational. Physically, I'm in great shape. Emotionally, I feel whole. I meditate regularly, and I'm a certified yoga teacher. Practicing yoga has taught me self-acceptance and how to understand the meaning and definition of yoga—a science of the mind. I chose to become a yoga teacher for my personal development, and I had two goals: to become a better listener and master the art of equanimity.

I believe words like inner self, self-awareness, and meditation belong in this heart-centered leadership book. When we lead from the inside, we are genuinely heart-centered and fully aligned—body, mind, and soul—because we have self-acceptance. Leading from the inside is knowing who we are and having strong self-awareness we never waiver from, especially in difficult times.

Listening to my inner self, knowing that I maintain that innate young-girl outlook of being the best person I can be each day, is peaceful and calming. Spiritually, I stay open to continual learning, embracing the new, and letting go of what no longer serves me.

Mentally, I feel completely integrated. I don't worry about what people think of me, and I compete with only myself. I know who I am. I like who I am. I am no longer a doormat for others.

This next idea encompasses stepping into your greatness, shining your light, and confidently expressing your core beliefs and values: *It's not your job to like me. It's mine.*

How can we link together midlife wisdom and the science of our mind?

A great example of a heart-centered entrepreneur is hotelier Chip Conley. After he sold his hotel conglomerate, the entrepreneur extraordinaire was looking for a midlife change. That's when the brain team behind Airbnb reached out. They wanted his maturity and experience.

At first, he wondered who would want to rent someone else's home when they could make a reservation at a nice hotel. Now, Chip has taken Airbnb to the stratosphere and Chip himself learned that along the way to middle age, it's vital to keep our youthful curiosity and imagination alive. Chip has coined a new term for middle age: modern elder. The Airbnb owners reminded him that he'd lost his curiosity and imagination while building his business (Crowe 2022). Chip also opened the Modern Elder Academy, which has people from around the globe visit and realize their purpose. He is taking his current term as elder far and wide (Locker 2018).

One way to link midlife wisdom and the science of our minds is by exploring how our brains change with age and how this affects our decision-making, emotional regulation, and overall well-being. By understanding the science behind these changes, we can gain insights into how to cultivate wisdom and resilience during midlife and beyond. Michael Netzley's company is lightyears ahead in their research on how our brains improve with age (Netzley 2021).

For me, experiences have shaped this link. Trauma, loss, disappointment—all these negative experiences helped me realize that I've been emotionally resilient since losing my father at age twenty-one.

Now a modern elder, I recognize that emotional intelligence has become my default coping toolkit. Not having support or knowing where to find it so early on in life was pivotal for me. My inner being grew strong knowing I could always cry without feeling lost, pick myself up, and find a way to start again.

This solid inner faith has been a power in my life; I know I can always restart without self-judgment or being emotionally swayed by other people's unkind words or actions.

The lesson that took me the longest to learn was to not allow poor treatment or disrespect from others. Even if it's a job contract, people-pleasing is exhausting—and people will take advantage of you if you allow it. Power lies in confidently stepping forward and knowing and loving who you are. I've always loved the acronym FLY. My favorite interpretation: "First Love Yourself."

Volunteering in our city at St. Joseph's Hospice for several years was a humbling experience—it's an honor to be with someone at the end of life. My listening skills grew, the stories I heard were priceless, and the memories will last a lifetime.

In April 2016, I started in the community with a wonderful woman named JJ. She was a teacher throughout her career, then retired and soon became ill. We met every Wednesday afternoon at her beautiful home. I genuinely believe we were meant to meet and be together. I knew that, eventually, she would be fully admitted into hospice care, which happened in June. On the evening of her admission, the oncologist shared that he didn't think she would last the night, but JJ had other plans. Not only did she settle well into hospice, but she also awoke the following day feeling ready to dance! The oncologist had no explanation.

JJ lived for eighty-eight days in hospice. She was known for plastering yellow happy faces all over her room. Everyone remembers her to this day—because she brought a level of joy the hospice needed. JJ passed away in September, and I had the honor and privilege of giving the eulogy at her funeral.

From 1990 to 2010, I owned and managed a medical-rehabilitation practice. I started it as a home-based business, and ultimately, in 2005, I moved to a lovely clinic in our city. I sat on the floor of my new office and looked at all the boxes. Tears streamed down my face as I looked up, talking to my dad.

I felt like I had "made it," despite not quite knowing what that meant.

From 2005 to 2010, my business grew exponentially, and I eventually had a staff of four. It was one of the busiest and most rewarding times of my life. I was a working mom-entrepreneur—married with two young girls, ages nine and seven. I also traveled a lot. All of this meant that organizing, structuring, and planning were critical strategies. Some of my most-cherished activities when I came home were cooking meals and baking with the girls. It was a de-stressing strategy for me, and I told them stories of Nana.

I also spent many years testifying in court for my catastrophic clients who had sustained traumatic brain or spinal cord injuries. It was exhausting to prepare, testify, and give my best effort to convince the jury how catastrophic these people were. Ultimately, the insurance companies and lawyers grew more prosperous, and I questioned whether I wanted to remain in the insurance industry.

Then, in 2010, a disability insurance company called to ask if I would take on five short-term disability claims. The adjudicator said, "I heard you're great at getting people back to work."

What I didn't realize was that these new short-term disability claims were about to give me a gentle nudge toward navigating a powerful life lesson. I was assigned five executives: two CEOs and three VPs. They were all on a short-term disability claim for stress. They thought they had it all—yet they were lonely and unhealthy, had failed in their marriages, and had tumultuous relationships with their children and grandchildren.

Their short-term disability claims became long-term very quickly, and then all five executives were diagnosed with palliative treatment and in hospice.

I sat with them at the end of their lives, and each was indeed a heartfelt moment. As I held their hands, they cried and shared how their life choices had made them unhappy and sick. They were chasing status and had lost much in life as they continued to climb the ladder of success. They shared that they would die with many untold stories still inside.

The defining moment for me was realizing they all had the same two regrets from their leadership journey: They had failed to speak up when they should have, and they tolerated a toxic culture.

After, my mind reeled from knowing and spending time with these five executives. From the start of their disability claim to the moment of their passing away was ten months, and I felt immense loss and grief.

The regrets they shared played over and over in my mind. I had promised them I would do something about it, although I didn't know what that might be. However, I chose to lean in, think, feel, and look to the future for a solution.

A week later, I had a coaching session with my executive coach. He asked what I was thinking of doing next in my business, and I was at a loss for words.

"Those executives opened a doorway for you," he said.

His remark dumbfounded me. I didn't understand its intent. So, he explained that I could help save so many future leaders at all levels. Having a medical-rehabilitation background gave me a great foundation to meet them at exactly where they were in life and their leadership journey; he also alluded to my helping get them holistically back on track.

This was pivotal: our leadership journey brings transferrable skills, moments, and experiences into whatever we choose next on our life journey. For the next eighteen months I worked to become a certified executive life and leadership coach, and I haven't looked back since that day.

My new coaching practice unfolded as it was meant to be. I love reminiscing and writing this to you in my heart-centered leadership playbook because we all have a powerful story to tell, and this is mine. I hope it sparks your curiosity, wisdom, and imagination to write your personal heart-centered leadership playbook.

Midlife, so often seen as a crisis, can also be viewed as a growth opportunity. It is a stage in which we may experience a profound sense of questioning, reflection, and transition. But while it can be unsettling and accompanied by feelings of restlessness or dissatisfaction, a midlife "crisis" offers a chance for personal exploration, self-discovery, and transformation. It prompts individuals to reevaluate their values, priorities, and goals, ultimately leading to a deeper inner understanding.

This period can serve as a catalyst for change, encouraging individuals to make positive shifts in their careers, relationships, and overall lifestyles. Embracing this transitional phase with openness and curiosity can pave the way for self-actualization and a renewed sense of purpose in the second half of life. By navigating the challenges and opportunities presented during midlife, individuals can emerge with greater self-awareness, resilience, and fulfillment.

The midlife wisdom you may be searching for is inside you. Stepping into greatness takes courage. Let go of the fear, step into the courage, and show the world your greatness.

Don't worry about what other people may think or say about you. You can't please everyone, and why would you want to? The best way to diet is by losing the weight of other people's opinions.

It's time to surrender. Open your heart and permit yourself to move on. Join me in being heart-centered in life and leadership.

FULL-CIRCLE LIFE MOMENT:
I've always known from a young age who I was. I failed to see that I allowed other people to decrease my value. My value now is limitless—I have mastered the art of heart in my own life and know that heart-centered leadership is the only way to lead and be.

♥

Wherever you go,
go with all your heart.

—CONFUCIUS

♥

CHAPTER 6

LEADERSHIP IN THE WAKE OF TRAGEDY

How can we lead with compassion and resilience in the face of tragedy?

By exploring the role of leadership during times of crisis, we can create a work environment that supports and empowers your team members.

(This is a true story. The names have been changed to protect patient identity.)

That moment in time: The phone call, the personal injury lawyer's voice, and the stillness that came over me in my office. In May 2004, a GMC Suburban struck two children in a strip-mall parking lot. But the phone call did not come until September.

Working in the medical rehabilitation sector came with excitement, gratitude, observation, and, sometimes, frustrating delay due to politics between insurance companies and the people they selected to work with injured people. This greatly upset me, as I often felt like the "sloppy second" choice—being given injured people's cases only after many of their claims had been neglected, along with their physical and mental health.

I met David and Elizabeth on a September afternoon. Elizabeth was a high-school student, working after school in the daycare her younger brother David attended. She would finish school, walk to the daycare to work and, afterward, collect David. They'd sit on the bench in front of the strip mall, waiting for their mother, Rachel, to pick them up and go home for dinner.

One day, Elizabeth took David into the nearby convenience store for a treat. As they returned to sit on the bench, she heard a loud noise and saw a large steel truck coming at her at high speed. She instinctively picked up her brother and threw him out of the way.

Moments later, their mother, Rachel, pulled into the parking lot and was faced with fire trucks, flashing red lights, and police cars. The noise pierced her ears as smoke, along with other pungent odors, filled the air.

She immediately got out of her car and asked a police officer what had happened. He told her that a GMC Suburban had struck two children. Instantly, and without thinking, she knew they were hers. She screamed their names and frantically started looking around and inside the truck. She saw part of Elizabeth's foot and screamed again—she was pinned under the vehicle. Her left leg was over her head and against the muffler, and her screams were unbearable. The firefighters were hosing down the truck to cool it down, while navigating a plan to lift the vehicle and remove Elizabeth.

A doctor came running to the scene from a neighboring medical clinic. He gave Rachel two pills to help calm her. The level of shock was immeasurable. She asked the first responders where David was, but no one had seen him. She ran through the parking lot screaming his name, then saw a minuscule figure on an enormous cement planter some eighty feet from the truck. She ran to her toddler son.

What happened next was the most challenging part for Rachel. Her daughter was removed from under the vehicle and taken by ambulance to the nearest hospital with extensive injuries. The paramedics worked on her unresponsive son who was sent to a different hospital.

As the ambulance carrying Elizabeth pulled away from the scene, Rachel collapsed on the ground.

Eventually, the police took her to Elizabeth's hospital. There, the ER doctor told Rachel that her daughter had second- and third-degree burns on the back of her left leg, extensive orthopedic injuries, and neurotrauma. They medicated her to manage the pain and stabilized her to prioritize a treatment plan. But at that point, a female police officer grabbed her arm and urged her to get into the car to go to her son. Rachel was not ready for what happened next.

As she entered the ER at the city's other hospital, her son was being worked on by the trauma team—but the doctor looked at Rachel and said he didn't think David would live. Within the next few seconds, a trauma team arrived from Detroit Children's Hospital. They were there to pick up a noncritical preemie baby for transfer from Canada across the border to the United States.

Dr. Sandeep Sood, a neurosurgeon from India, had moved to Detroit with his wife (also a neurosurgeon). When he arrived for the preemie, he saw David and told the doctor they would take him and return for the baby. Time was of the essence.

The United States can be entered from Canada by bridge or tunnel, the latter of which was closed at the time. The international ambulance ride took twelve minutes from door-to-door, with Dr. Sood leading the way to David's treatment.

David quickly underwent neurosurgery, and Dr. Sood saved his life.

Rachel sat in her kitchen drinking coffee, smoking cigarettes, and shaking. She had two injured children at two different hospitals in two different countries. When I received that fateful September phone call, she gave me a review of the timeline since the accident in May. She was a woman who had been in and out of cabs for four months, going from one hospital to another.

The day we met in person, I listened and wrote in point form to ensure I did not miss any vital facts or information. Rachel kept asking why her first case manager hadn't done anything, and I would gently redirect the conversation back to her children and assured her I would do my best to get the treatment they needed.

She described her experience of the last few months with tears rolling down her face, saying, "I have never been so medicated and unaware."

The doctor had put her on so many medications that—while present in her physical body, sitting with me—she was emotionally often somewhere else in her thoughts. She was cognitively exhausted, and much of the treatment was a blur. Her middle son, William, was being bounced from family to friends, as Rachel was a single parent to her three children.

I was physically and mentally exhausted when I left our initial home visit, a two-hour drive from my clinic. This new referral involving two catastrophically injured children would be a lot of work—a family of four to care for and case manage. That week, I started developing medical rehabilitation teams in Canada for Elizabeth and in the United States for David. It was a huge undertaking, and I knew I had to be on my game strategically and prepared for a lot of travel and communication with two large teams.

But there was no way to be ready for the unprofessionalism of the insurance claims adjuster.

I called her to introduce myself; she was curt, cold, and unhappy. She informed me that I was not her chosen case manager and refused to pay for my travel time (an action outside her domain). I listened intently and remained calm, as I was focused on securing the best care and treatment. There was a long road ahead to transition a toddler back from the United States to Canada. The key to the tone of this claim was to control myself and hone the quality of equanimity when speaking, writing, or communicating with this adjuster.

She attempted to make my involvement a problem for the following year, challenging every treatment recommendation as well as any suggested aids. I did not see an ounce of care from her; she was focused on saving the insurance company money, putting up barriers to my involvement, and doing everything she could to delay the progression of rehabilitation for these children.

Irritated, but calm and determined, I organized a large rehabilitation team meeting. This was the new team I had assembled in Canada for Elizabeth as well as for David. I worked with the US medical rehab in-patient team and wanted a smooth transition to Canada before bringing him home to his family. Rachel cared for Elizabeth at home while traveling daily to the other hospital by taxi to see David together while balancing William's life—all at the same time and alone.

On the day of the meeting, I drove to pick up Rachel. She was extremely nervous, as the adjuster had not been kind to her and now, they'd be coming face-to-face. I assured Rachel she could sit beside me and encouraged her to listen and not speak. I would facilitate the meeting.

As the new team assembled, the tone of the room was light but had a cloud of tension brewing. Rebecca, the adjuster, entered. She wore jeans and a black leather jacket; I was taken aback by her unprofessional dress code. The rest of us had dressed professionally. Then she threw a significant file on the ground, sat down, put her feet on it as her footstool, exhaled, and crossed her arms in front of her chest. As she breathed out, a pungent smell of cigarettes filled the air.

I took a deep breath and knew the journey would now begin. This was my time to be strategic and open the meeting with intent—to highlight my heart-centered leadership, and step into my greatness to the best of my knowledge and ability.

That is precisely what I did.

It was an hour-long opening. I ran a well-organized agenda and redirected when needing to keep to the structure and time. Rebecca did not comment nor move her feet to look at her file. After the meeting, I approached her to shake her hand and thank her for coming. She did not extend her hand but simply grabbed her leather coat and left the room without a goodbye.

Later in the car, Rachel asked how I thought the meeting was going. I shared that I felt confident in the team I had selected, that her children would get the best medical rehabilitation, and that her life would take on some semblance of normalcy going forward.

The next four years working with Rebecca on the case were not fun. She kept throwing barriers at every suggestion for the children. On a phone call one day, she said she did not like me and hadn't picked me to work on these two claims. Again, I felt sorry for her having such anger and resentment and knew it had nothing to do with me.

Going into the fifth year of this claim, I received a call from an adjuster named Christine. She explained that the insurance company would transfer cases every so often to give them new life and an objective set of eyes. It was a friendly, warm, and welcoming call. Christine asked me why I had never been paid travel time in almost five years. I explained that my relationship with Rebecca was complicated and that she had refused to pay me. I worked for these children, and I would invoice the insurance company for my time when I had time. I also explained that I ran my company with a people-over-profit mentality and knew I would be reimbursed eventually.

She thanked me for my patience and magnificent work on the claims. Then she said, "I'm paying you for all your travel plus interest. I'm embarrassed about how my colleague treated you, and I want to say sorry on behalf of our company."

I smiled (though she couldn't see it) and thanked her, and we said goodbye. I sat at my desk, tears streaming down my face. My patience, equanimity, and professionalism had led me here.

Being a heart-centered leader during a tragedy requires compassion, empathy, and the ability to provide support and guidance to those affected.

Here are some strategies you can consider.

1. Show genuine empathy: Connect with the emotions of those affected by the tragedy. Listen actively and demonstrate genuine care and concern. Acknowledge

their pain and validate their feelings, allowing them to express themselves openly.

2. Communicate openly and honestly: Be transparent in your communication with those affected. Provide accurate information about the situation, its impact, and any ongoing efforts to address the tragedy. Avoid withholding or sugarcoating information, as doing so can lead to mistrust and further distress.

3. Offer support and resources: Identify immediate needs and provide support accordingly. This could involve coordinating access to medical assistance, counseling services, financial aid, or any other necessary resources. Be proactive in seeking assistance for those in distress.

4. Foster a safe and inclusive environment: Create a space where individuals feel safe to share their experiences, concerns, and emotions. Encourage open dialogue and active listening among team members, promoting an atmosphere of support and understanding.

5. Lead by example: Demonstrate resilience, compassion, and self-care to inspire and motivate others. By taking care of your own well-being, you set an example for your team and show that it's essential to prioritize self-care during difficult times.

6. Encourage teamwork and collaboration: Facilitate opportunities for individuals to come together and support one another. Foster a sense of community and encourage teamwork to overcome challenges collectively. Encourage the sharing of ideas and solutions to help bounce back from the tragedy.

7. Provide opportunities for healing: Recognize the importance of healing and recovery. Offer access to counseling or therapy services, organize support groups,

or promote wellness activities that can help individuals cope with their emotions and regain their strength.

8. Adapt to changing needs: Tragedies can have long-lasting effects on individuals and communities. Stay attuned to the evolving needs of those affected and be flexible in adjusting your leadership approach. Regularly assess the situation and adapt your strategies as required.

Being a heart-centered leader means prioritizing the well-being and emotional needs of those affected. Your actions should reflect compassion, empathy, and a genuine desire to support and uplift others during these challenging times.

It's important to note that each family situation is unique, and families should seek professional guidance tailored to their specific circumstances.

The road to recovery after a brain injury like David's can be long and challenging, but with patience, resilience, and a strong support system, families can help their loved ones navigate this journey.

FULL-CIRCLE LIFE MOMENT:
We learn from tragedy. Reflecting on the mistakes, shortcomings, and consequences that led to the tragedy helps us in our leadership. Through introspection and analysis, we can identify areas where leadership could have been improved or where decisions could have been made differently.

By acknowledging these lessons, heart-centered leaders can develop a deeper understanding of the impact their actions and decisions have on people's lives—then use that knowledge to make wiser choices in the future. Ultimately, learning from tragedy allows heart-centered leaders to grow, adapt, and develop better strategies to prevent similar incidents from occurring and to guide their teams with greater empathy, wisdom, and effectiveness.

♥

Kind words can be short
and easy to speak,
but their echoes are truly endless.

—MOTHER TERESA

♥

CHAPTER 7

MY IRISH NANA

How can the wisdom and love of an elder impact our approach to life and leadership?

Investigate the distinctive contributions that grandmothers and other modern elders can make in influencing our perspective and shaping our core beliefs and principles. From their stories and experiences, we can learn timeless lessons on compassion, empathy, and resilience that can transform the way we lead and live.

Discover how the influence of an elder can ripple out into the world and make a lasting impact on those around us.

In my case, my Irish Nana set the foundation for my beliefs and morals. She taught me that not all people would be kind— but nevertheless, I always have the opportunity to pause and control how I respond to them and navigate each situation.

Born in 1966, I was the youngest of five children. I had three older brothers and one older sister. My mother used to tell me my birth was not planned and that I was not like my other siblings.

From a young age, I knew I was destined to be something great. My father, an entrepreneur, was not home often, while my mother was the model of a good housewife.

She dressed nicely each day, and the house was spotless. The children were kept clean and quiet, and meals were always on time, especially dinner. We were to be seen but not heard when my father arrived home. Dinner was served, condiments and all. There was no choice; we ate dinner or went to our rooms. I was a skinny kid and spent much time alone in my room.

As children, we wanted for nothing extrinsically and had everything money could buy. We had a lovely, clean home and took vacations every year. But the maternal, loving mother one might expect was absent.

Her days consisted of the usual cleaning routine, taking cigarette breaks, ensuring her kids were not dirty, cleaning more, then calling her friends at three in the afternoon. Sometimes, the neighborhood wives club assembled in our kitchen to watch their favorite soap operas, have cocktails, and chain-smoke until it was time for them to go home and prepare dinner for their families.

It was 1968. I was two years old and standing in my wooden playpen in the living room. Being a toddler and seeing what was happening around me was thrilling. I was bright and alert, and through my nonverbal communication and intuition, I knew that what my blue eyes were seeing was not correct.

This early childhood experience secured the understanding in my soul that I deserved better. While having a photographic memory can be both a blessing and a curse, those vivid childhood memories have become lessons of gratitude and shaped the person I am today: A middle-aged modern elder, full of appreciation and unique stories of how that appreciation came to be and how I learned at an early age to enjoy my own company and quiet solitude.

It has been said that life is not about the number of breaths you take but the moments that take your breath away. My Nana was one of the few who truly had a wonderful life. She was the voice that never failed to give us the comfort we needed and the best advice.

A woman of principle and courage, she stood firmly for what she believed. It's from her that I've learned to stay strong. Moreover, she was also a woman with a gentle smile and a soothing voice. At home, she hummed and sang the lyrics of a favorite song in a faltering voice.

I often walked in on Nana chattering with my grandfather, who was alive in her heart but no longer in this world. She would look at me and giggle, and I'd pretend I hadn't heard.

She loved pastel colors, eating fish and chips, and enjoying hot tea—all those little memorable things. During my reminiscences, I know that, in the end, what we remember best are not the grand gestures but all the tiny, essential bits of a person's character.

There's only so much my emotional capacity can handle as I remember her. It would be enough to say that having her in my life was a blessing. She taught me what it meant to be alive and to love, and filled a space in me that my parents never could.

Nana was born in Liverpool, England, on March 11, 1908. I idolized her from birth but started to really remember her vividly from age three. English-born, with strong Irish roots— she was my role model in life, and my second mother. We had an extraordinary bond; she brought out the best in me.

She loved to be called Lil and played a mean game of Euchre. When she drank, it had to be dark rum and Coke. In December, though, it would be rum and eggnog to celebrate Christmas.

One of the best life experiences she gave me was taking me to church. She created my love of faith and all aspects of life and taught me that God is always with me during good and bad times. All I had to do was ask for his help, guidance, and direction. I was never alone. This was an epiphany for me. Back at home, I felt alone most of the time.

Nana was an intelligent woman in possession of many beautiful traits. She was brilliant and had a fantastic sense of humor. But, most importantly, she taught me to accept people with disabilities. As a young girl, she had been diagnosed with polio in her right leg. The doctors in England wanted to amputate her leg, but my great-grandmother, Alice, would not allow it. Instead, the family immigrated to Canada. They sailed across the Atlantic Ocean and moved to Toronto, Ontario.

The doctors did not have to amputate her leg. It was inordinately small—the size of a wrist—and she strolled, as her foot was crooked, and her toes had to be fused. None of this slowed her down; in fact, she frequently joked about it. Her feet were different sizes, so she hated shoe shopping. When she walked, she led with her left leg while her right leg and foot dragged behind.

To Nana, this was not a disability. She demonstrated that she could do anything: she put her mind to it, and it would be done. Her bad leg was nicknamed her "gammy leg," and we laughed about it.

From age nine until my teen years, we spent every weekend together. Nana would pick me up and take me to her house, and I loved it. When I got home on Sunday night, I'd dump my suitcase into my hamper and repack it for the following Friday right away. Then I'd count five more nights of sleep until I was back at Nana's.

I thank God she was in my life, shaping my character during the most challenging years. She taught me simple yet necessary core values; she called it common sense. If we treat people the way we want to be treated, we will never go wrong. To this day, I have never wavered from this core belief.

Nana enhanced my entrepreneurial skills as well. My older siblings received one dollar per week allowance from her. One day, I tried to persuade her to consider inflation and raise my weekly allowance to two dollars. She laughed and shook her head.

Although I had a biological mother, Nana, in my eyes and heart, was my true mother. I still think about our weekends and all the beautiful memories we created together. She gave me a love of baking and cooking, plus a genuine appreciation of our cultural roots in England and Ireland.

Sometimes she'd travel to Ireland to see relatives, and I always loved the smell of her suitcase when she came home and opened it. To me, it smelled like the ocean.

When she stopped driving, we walked everywhere or took the city bus. My favorite adventures were always on Sundays. As we walked to church, I'd skip alongside her, chattering, and carrying on while she smiled and hoped my energy would be used up before we arrived.

We also played together and often had tea parties with freshly baked goods. She showed me how to roll the homemade dough with her arthritic hands while we chatted and sang or listened to her favorite music. Our best snack with tea were her famous "jam buddies."

The single best attribute that I possess today, and one for which I'm so grateful, is the voice I have—because Nana taught me to speak up and be heard. She taught me to be who I am and not to be fearful. She showered me with love and affection and told me I would do great things.

Nana's hearing declined as she aged, and she eventually had to wear hearing aids. As I write, memories around this have me laughing out loud. While we sat in church, she'd adjust the volume setting to hear the minister and enjoy the choir. Her hearing aids would whistle away, her "gammy leg" tapping on the floor, as if she had a grand old time. I'd elbow her gently and gesture to lower the volume, and she'd nod, laughing softly.

My father was busy with work and regularly uprooted our family. In fact, we didn't live in any home for more than two years. The first time we moved, I had just started kindergarten and begun to develop my social circle, but I didn't get very far. By the time first grade began, I was already at a new school and living in the country on a farm, starting over again. That land was my safe ground, my favorite place. We had a dog, rabbits, horses, cattle, ducks, and one hundred acres of gorgeous outdoors where I could roam, run, sing, dance, and play. We spent the next two years at the farm, and I loved it.

At age nine, we moved back to the city into a semi-detached home. I treated every move as an adventure; I am imaginative, and my young mind thought I should view it as a positive. It was the best way to deal with moving, as I had no choice. I loved my new L-shaped room, and my closet was the coolest. But after this move, my life changed forever.

Each day, when I arrived home, my mother maintained her cocktail hour. She had to do it alone, though, as she had yet to meet a new circle of friends. She was shy and, perhaps, not very good at making friends—so she didn't really try to meet new people. By then, my siblings were older and had their own lives and independence. My oldest brother was married and starting life with his new wife.

I genuinely longed to have a close bond with my mother, full of maternal wisdom, affection, and playfulness. It was only a dream for me, but the voice that changed everything came to my rescue: my father's mother, Elizabeth Gertrude Martin. Nana was always there at the right time and moment.

Relocating so often was difficult for me as a child because I never felt settled anywhere. The inconsistency of developing and sustaining friendships was problematic, and I never seemed to have enough time to be with my new friends. This made me feel that I didn't have a sense of belonging or a social foundation. An outlier was how I felt—a true vagabond.

Then, in 1987, my dad passed away at the age of fifty-four. Nana and I stayed at the hospital around-the-clock for almost a week that September; he passed away in the early hours of a Sunday morning. It was beyond heartbreaking; I was twenty-one and had to watch Nana lose her only child, something no parent should ever experience. After my dad's passing, I felt lost and didn't know where my life was headed. The old cliché that tells us time heals all wounds is true. We kept his memory alive by chatting about him, telling stories, and celebrating his life. My life as a young adult carried on.

Sometime after that, Nana loaned me money to buy my first new car, a 1988 Pontiac Firefly, and celebrated with me. I adored this car. It was light gray with four doors, a hatchback, and a sunroof. It even had a stereo and a cassette player. This was a vast, positive milestone in my life, and once again, Nana was there to share it with me.

On May 30, 1990, I started my own company. My dad's name was David William; to honor him and keep his entrepreneurial spirit alive, I named it Davwill Consulting, Inc.

While living in my apartment in 1992, I worked with many contract clients and my life took shape. At that time, Nana lived with my sister in Port Dover, Ontario, a ninety-minute drive from where I lived in London, Ontario. We talked on the phone and wrote letters back and forth, and I tried to see her every couple of months.

Also, around this time, I had been dating a man named John Crowe and was very fond of him. In 1991, he asked me to marry him, and with great excitement, I visited Nana and showed her my engagement ring. She was equally excited, and we discussed wedding plans—the date was set for September 18, 1993. I envisioned Nana sitting in the front pew of the church and could not wait to have her share that moment with us.

In December 1992, my mother, older brother, and his family visited Nana for the last time. I asked to go with them, but the weather was terrible, and they didn't have room in the car for me, so I wasn't able to see her. Four days later, Nana passed away. My heart was broken that day: December 17, 1992.

My best friend, confidant, and substitute mother had gone to be with the Lord, and I was overwhelmed with sadness to the point of feeling ill. I still deeply regret not seeing her, hugging her, or saying goodbye.

There was always a funny story with Nana, even in her passing. She had told me she would pass away in her sleep—and was true to her word. She was innately organized and had all her affairs in order: her bed could be adjusted to prop her up comfortably so she could watch television in her bedroom, and she had her tea caddy situated beside her.

My sister usually checked on her before she went to bed. However, on this night, she did not. Nana had all this divinely crafted. She passed away quietly in her sleep, and my sister told me how peaceful she looked when she entered her room. She was eighty-four years old.

After, I went to church and arranged a celebration service for Nana and her remarkable life. I wrote and gave the eulogy. The priest was comforting and supportive and said he was honored to have me participate in the celebration. Nana had been cremated, and we brought her ashes to the church and put them up front for everyone to see.

There was a large gathering of people who adored and loved her. I gave one of the best speeches of my life, honoring a woman who was always there for me and had significantly impacted who I am. Through laughter and tears, Nana helped me develop and appreciate life one step at a time. My eulogy conveyed what a rich and whole life she had lived. She learned from her mistakes and, most importantly, always carried on.

When the service ended, we had a lovely luncheon at one of her favorite restaurants, where we laughed, cried, and reminisced with family and friends. In my opinion, keeping a loved one's memory alive is how you honor them. When I'm troubled, confused, or curious, I ask Nana for guidance—for her to give me a sign. She conveniently complies by leaving a nickel coin for me to find. Every time I ask her a question, a nickel appears. Then there are days when I'm working in my home office, and I can smell her Chanel No. 5 perfume, or her Oil of Olay, as though she were in the next room. I genuinely believe she's with me.

I have a picture of her above my home office desk and another of her with her mother, Alice, on her wedding day. You may say I've not let her out of my sight; she is with me daily. I am who I am today because of this extraordinary woman I am blessed to have had as a nana.

On my wedding day, I followed the tradition of something old, new, borrowed, and blue. Nana once gave me a beautiful handkerchief from Ireland that had embroidered blue flowers on it. I wrapped that handkerchief around the base of my flower bouquet and held it close to me. She was there in spirit, holding my hand.

LEARNING TO LEAD

Learning to lead without the support of family or mentors can certainly be challenging—but it is not impossible.

Below are some heart-centered strategies you can take to develop your leadership skills.

1. Define your leadership style: Start by understanding your own values, strengths, and weaknesses. Reflect on the qualities you admire in leaders and the kind of leader you want to become. This self-awareness will provide a foundation for further development.
2. Read books and study leadership: There is a wealth of knowledge available in books written by successful leaders. Read biographies, self-help books, and leadership literature to gain insights and learn from the experiences of others. Some books on leadership I recommend include *The 21 Irrefutable Laws of Leadership* by John C. Maxwell,

Primal Leadership by Daniel Goleman, and *Leaders Eat Last* by Simon Sinek.

3. Look online: In today's digital age, numerous online resources and courses can help you develop leadership skills. Look for webinars, podcasts, TED Talks, and online courses specifically focused on leadership development. Websites like Coursera, Udemy, and LinkedIn Learning offer a variety of options.

4. Find virtual mentors: Although you may not have direct access to mentors in your immediate circle, you can seek virtual ones. Follow thought leaders, successful entrepreneurs, and executives on social media platforms like LinkedIn, Twitter, or YouTube. Engage with their content, ask questions, and seek their guidance indirectly.

5. Join heart-centered, leadership-oriented communities: Look for spaces that focus on heart-centered leadership development. Attend related conferences, seminars, or workshops. Engage with like-minded individuals and build a network of peers who are also interested in leadership growth.

6. Embrace opportunities: Look for chances to take on leadership roles or projects within your current environment, such as at work, in volunteer organizations, or even in informal group settings. Taking initiative and demonstrating heart-centered leadership qualities will help you gain practical experience and refine your skills.

7. Reflect and learn from experiences: Actively seek feedback from others and reflect on your own actions and outcomes. Learn from both successes and failures to continuously improve your heart-centered leadership abilities. Journaling can be a helpful tool for self-reflection and personal growth.

8. Practice empathy and active listening: Effective heart-centered leadership requires understanding and connecting

with others. Practice empathy by putting yourself in others' shoes and actively listening to their perspectives.

9. Continuously develop yourself: Heart-centered leadership is a lifelong journey. Keep learning and growing by staying up to date with the latest trends and best practices. Regularly assess your progress, set goals, and take steps to further develop your leadership skills.

Remember, heart-centered leadership is not solely dependent on having a mentor or family support. It requires self-motivation, dedication, and continuous learning. By following these steps and remaining persistent, you can develop yourself into an effective leader.

FULL-CIRCLE LIFE MOMENT:

Value the time you have with yourself. Tap into your inner voice and emotions to find what you want from life. For example, I love being by myself. Most people are surprised when I tell them I am an INFJ, an initialism used in the publications of the Myers–Briggs Type Indicator to refer to one of the sixteen personality types. It stands for Introversion (I), Intuition (N), Feeling (F), and Judgment (J). This personality type is rare, making up less than one percent of the population, but they nonetheless leave their mark on the world.

There is not a "one-size-fits-all" assessment. We are all individual in our thoughts, feeling, emotions and behavior.

Life is a gift. Gratitude is priceless. Learning moments build character. Patience is a virtue. Each day is a fresh new start.

♥

The thing that lies at the foundation of
positive change, the way I see it,
is service to a fellow human being.

—LEE IACOCCA

♥

CHAPTER 8

HEART-CENTERED LEADERSHIP QUALITIES

What are the qualities that define a truly heart-centered leader?

From empathy and authenticity to mindfulness and gratitude, we'll delve into the core values and behaviors that can help you create a work environment where everyone feels valued, respected, and empowered.

Unlock the power of your heart and become the kind of leader who inspires greatness in others.

In January 2020, I created the heart-centered leadership qualities sketch note. It was originally intended to help leaders at all levels navigate our uncertain world during a global pandemic.

These twenty qualities are based on my observation and work as an entrepreneur since 1990 but are not meant to be a comprehensive list. This is a baseline and an invitation to start being attentive to the qualities you feel you have now and those you would like to develop.

When a leader can share their top three qualities within their heart-centered leadership skillsets, then declare the one quality they are working on, it allows for an intrinsic approach within teams and organizations.

I have witnessed this firsthand in coaching, with leaders at all levels from many different sectors as well as in facilitating team-building sessions in large organizations.

When the leader leans in and declares their top three qualities, and then leans in with further vulnerability to declare the one they've chosen to work on—that is where the magic happens.

I've observed numerous sighs of relief and enthusiastic affirmations of "Me too!" when we openly share our daily experiences, reveal our top three heart-centered qualities, and honestly acknowledge the one quality we are actively improving, it truly fosters a sense of connection, authenticity, and a strong sense of community among us.

The qualities we possess change daily. This is why leaders learn and evolve daily. It's a lifelong process. Our top three qualities will shift, as well as the one quality we may need or want to work on.

Crowe, Deborah. 2020. Heart-Centered Leadership Qualities. Ontario, CA: Deb Crowe.

This poster accompanies the heart-centered leadership card deck for effective team building below.

This document has traveled around the world and is now in twenty-five languages. Flip to the Resources section to learn how to download your own copy.

THE HEART-CENTERED LEADERSHIP QUALITIES CARD DECK

TRUTHFUL

In leadership, being truthful is not easy; it can also, at times, be seen as a weakness. But I can share with you that it's one of the best qualities you can have as a heart-centered leader—and it is *not* a weakness.

Honest leaders are viewed as effective by employees. They keep everyone abreast of what is going on within the organization—good and bad. Being honest builds trust. And trust is one of the most critical elements within the ability to delegate, inspire, and communicate effectively—a vital element of company culture.

Heart-Centered Leadership

TRUTHFUL

©2021 BY DEB CROWE

"Leadership is not one specific element. Each leader brings uniqueness to their role. It is not their title, role, or responsibilities that make them great leaders. It's the sum of their lives, work, and academic experiences that offer them the ability to be a great leader."

How does being truthful show up in your leadership?

Is being truthful easily observed within your team?

Does your organizational culture have a solid foundation for being truthful?

Heart-Centered Leadership

TRUSTWORTHY

©2021 BY DEB CROWE

When your team trusts you as a leader, it increases their commitment to team goals.

When your team doesn't trust you, you do not get their best efforts. You won't be able to inspire, persuade, or make real change, leaving you an ineffective leader. Trust is the foundation of who you are and aligns with being Approachable.

What is the difference between truthful and trustworthy when it comes to heart-centered leadership?

"Truthful" refers to a person who tells the truth, while "trust-worthy" refers to a person who can be relied upon to keep their promises and maintain confidentiality.

In terms of heart-centered leadership, a truthful leader may be honest about their actions and intentions, while a trustworthy leader inspires confidence and loyalty in their followers.

"Trust is the currency of leadership. A leader who is trust-worthy earns the unwavering loyalty and commitment of their followers, for they know that their leader's words and actions are consistent and reliable."

How do you demonstrate that you are a trustworthy leader?

Are you able to observe the effect of being trustworthy on your team?

Is your organizational culture built from a place of being trustworthy?

Heart-Centered Leadership

MODELS SELF-CARE

©2021 BY DEB CROWE

When you take care of "you," it demonstrates a deep level of self-awareness. It also allows both communication/non-communication skills to be highlighted in a positive manner. When you allow room for white space (a.k.a., time off) in your calendar, you honor yourself. When shared with the team, it becomes team self-care. This is the foundation for maintaining a healthy, vital culture that fosters a Safe, Welcoming Environment.

"Once we realize that we are already found—already who we were meant to be—we can start the process of discovering and becoming who we really are."

How do you demonstrate that you are a leader who values self-care?

Are you able to both lead and mentor self-care for your team?

Is your organizational culture built from a place of being healthy and leading a vital life without burnout?

SERVANT LEADER

Servant leadership is a philosophy in which the goal of the leader is to serve. This is different from traditional leadership, in which the leader's focus is to grow their company or organization. Embrace the possibilities of people over profit, then allow this element of leadership to foster and grow the business acumen aspect of your role.

"It begins with the inherent desire to serve, the desire to serve first. Leadership must address the needs of others first and foremost. Nothing significant occurs without a dream. For something truly extraordinary to occur, a truly extraordinary dream is required."

How do you demonstrate that you are a leader who values people over profit?

Are you able to demonstrate and be a servant leader for your team?

Is your organizational culture built from a place of servant leadership?

Heart-Centered Leadership

OPEN-MINDED

©2021 BY DEB CROWE

Leaders who are open-minded tend to be more self-aware. An open-minded leader is prepared to enjoy new experiences or ideas, as they are attentive listeners and bring forth an intrinsic approach to their thinking. Alignment with Self-Care, Trustworthy, and Lifelong Learner.

"Intelligence is measured on how well you can adapt."

How do you demonstrate that you are a leader who values other peoples opinions?

Are you able to consistently demonstrate your ability to be an open-minded leader?

Is your organizational culture built from a place of being open-minded?

OWN CHARACTER

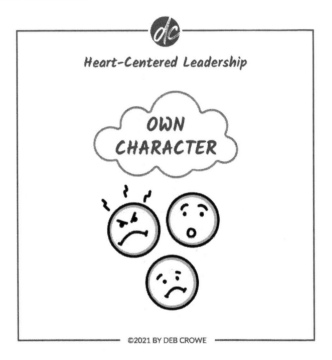

When you can fully own your character, you embrace an important level of authenticity as a leader. You are comfortable demonstrating your beliefs and values, and you take pride in doing so consistently. When you are authentic in owning your character, your leadership style exudes confidence, optimism, hope, and resilience. Aligned with Committed and Compassionate Toward Self and Others.

"There is no mental flaw that has resulted in as much resentment as people's tendency to ignore and forgive their own mistakes, no matter how egregious or how often they occur."

How do you demonstrate that you are a leader who values your own self-awareness?

Are you able to consistently demonstrate your ability to share your own character flaws?

Is your organizational culture built from a place of being honest and transparent?

This is the highest level of being open-minded and approachable. You can show and demonstrate that you are evolving as a leader, are humble enough to learn new ways of thinking, or are looking at something through someone else's eyes, and enjoying the view from the observer's chair. Alignment with Mindful of Words.

"At any age, whether twenty or eighty, a person who ceases to educate themselves is considered old. Learning is the key to eternal youth."

How do you demonstrate that you are a leader who continues to learn and grow?

Are you able to consistently demonstrate your ability to share what you are learning?

Is your organizational culture built from a place of continued learning to foster growth and progression?

AVID READER

Heart-Centered Leadership

AVID READER

©2021 BY DEB CROWE

Leaders have always been known as readers. Allowing yourself to keep the best business concepts in the forefront of your thoughts allows you to stay focused and disciplined with the company mission. It also helps to hone your vivid visionary skills, then apply the discipline and structure needed to keep the company moving forward. Leaders should have exposure to new and thoughtful ideas. Choose books that are insightful, and don't be afraid to read something outside the norm. Alignment with Responsible and Models Self-Care.

"Reading is the only way we can get into another person's body, voice, and spirit without meaning to and often without being able to help ourselves."

How do you demonstrate that you are a leader who values taking the time to read?

Are you able to consistently demonstrate your ability to share what you are reading?

Is your organizational culture built from a place of continued learning to foster professional development?

Heart-Centered Leadership

APPROACHABLE

©2021 BY DEB CROWE

Being approachable is a leadership skill that requires a daily audit to ensure you're not missing an opportunity or valuable information. Often, leaders get overloaded with information and are unaware of not being fully present or attentively listening. As a leader at any level, approach-ability matters. Become the leader with an open-door policy. Alignment with Servant Leadership, Empathetic, and Mindful of Words.

"There are people who think they should be with you but can't because of something."

How do you demonstrate that you are a leader who is approachable?

Are you able to consistently demonstrate your ability to be approachable with your team?

Is your organizational culture built from a place of openness and honesty to foster approachability?

STRATEGIST

Heart-Centered Leadership

STRATEGIST

©2021 BY DEB CROWE

Communication is one of your best assets when you are a strategist. You can articulate well. Strategic leaders must be able to communicate with clarity. Clarity comes from the art of honing equanimity. Strategic leaders *think* before acting or speaking and are cognizant of Attentive Listening. Also aligns with Mindful of Words.

"The greatest danger comes from taking no chances at all. When faced with rapid global change, the only plan guaranteed to fail is doing nothing. Everyone can see the methods by which I achieve triumph, but they cannot comprehend the strategy from which those methods are derived."

How do you demonstrate that you are a leader who is a visionary thinker?

Are you able to consistently demonstrate your ability to be forward-thinking with your team?

Is your organizational culture built from a place of vision that encompasses three, five, and seven years ahead?

Heart-Centered Leadership

HELPS OTHERS RISE & GIVE SUPPORT

©2021 BY DEB CROWE

As leaders, you can be seated in the foundation of the "big picture." It is in the moments of a conversation that helps you be decisive, compliment someone, and step into utilizing the art of intrinsic validation. When you notice and discover what's important to others, you align with Offer a Safe, Welcoming Environment. Plus, celebrating the success of your team is a direct alignment with Committed.

"Do good deeds for others not because of who they are or what they can do for you in return, but because it is the right thing to do."

How do you demonstrate that you are a leader who is always supportive of others?

Are you able to consistently demonstrate your ability to be supportive?

Is your organizational culture built from a place of vision that offers everyone opportunities to grow?

MINDFUL OF WORDS

Being mindful of your words is a foundational leadership skill. It means trying to lead without ego and being willing to put the interest of others before yourself. It also represents the ability to take an honest look at yourself through regularly aligning with Model Self-Care.

"Always think about what you say, because what you say shows what's in your heart."

How do you demonstrate that you are a leader who is always mindful of your communication?

Are you able to consistently demonstrate your ability to be mindful?

Is your organizational culture built from a place of being mindful?

Active listening can encourage stronger communication between you and your team members. The objective of this kind of listening is to fully understand the message, including *any feelings beyond the spoken word* that may be conveyed nonverbally. Alignment with Model Self-Care, Empathetic, and Mindful of Words.

"Since we only have one mouth and two ears, we should learn to use the latter more often. I've found that those who listen more than they speak tend to be the most successful."

How do you demonstrate that you are a leader who is always listening?

Are you able to consistently demonstrate your ability to be an exemplary listener?

Is your organizational culture built from a place of being both listened to and heard?

COMPASSIONATE FOR SELF AND OTHERS

This aligns with Models Self-Care. When demonstrated in your daily leadership activities, it allows for the self-expression of vulnerability, authenticity, and transparency. When you can take time to care, Servant Leader members of your team will never forget how you made them feel and that you possess being Approachable.

"A leader with compassion is driven by a desire to improve the lives of those under their charge, whether they are consumers, investors, suppliers, employees, the government, or communities. Compassionate leaders understand their constituents and speak to their worries, aspirations, and apprehensions."

How do you demonstrate that you are a leader who models and mentors compassion?

Are you able to consistently demonstrate your ability to be a compassionate leader?

Is your organizational culture built from a place of compassion?

The sector you work in (primary, secondary, or tertiary) is important. Given today's climate, we are now borderless and every leader is in the people business. Put simply, responsible leadership is about making sustainable business decisions that consider the interests of *all* people (including shareholders, employees, clients, suppliers, the community, the environment, and future generations). Alignment with Strategist, Ability to Fail Forward, Lifelong Learner.

"You are a leader if your actions inspire others to dream more, study more, do more, and become more. Measuring a leader's greatness is measured by the accomplishments of those whom the leader guides."

How do you demonstrate that you are a responsible leader?

Are you able to consistently demonstrate your ability to be responsible?

Is your organizational culture founded on mentoring, sustainability, and accountability?

COMMITTED

Being committed as a leader aligns with Lifelong Learner. Leadership characterized by commitment demonstrates devotion to a business and its people. Committed leaders put time into pursuing the organization's and team members' needs, to advance the organization's values and objectives.

Leaders need to spend time out of their offices to allow time to think, recharge, and invite the opportunity to be creative and innovative. They need to work and "roll their sleeves up" alongside their staff to appease anxieties and solicit input for improvements. Being committed to taking their ideas and transferring them across the company is the key. By listening to these ideas, a leader can establish relationships based on confidence and trust. They become a trusted advisor, demonstrating that continuous improvement is not only desired but adopted by their heart-centered leadership. Alignment with Trustworthy, Open-Minded, and being a Strategist.

"Motivate your team to fully invest in the project's success, not only participate in it."

How do you demonstrate that you are a leader who is committed to the people?

Are you able to consistently demonstrate your commitment?

Is your organizational culture founded on being committed?

Heart-Centered Leadership

OFFER A SAFE, WELCOMING ENVIRONMENT

©2021 BY DEB CROWE

This is one of the most important leadership functions today, given the modern world's various unknowns. Encourage your team to praise each other with simple gestures or kind words based on a job well done. Create an environment that is open and has equal communication.

"Leaders can and should try to create an environment where employees feel safe sharing personal thoughts and experiences at work. This is not a trait, but a characteristic of the workplace."

Are you demonstrating that you are a leader who always offers your team a safe, welcoming environment?

Are you able to consistently demonstrate your ability to ensure psychological safety?

Is your organizational culture founded on being and feeling safe, heard, seen, and validated?

ABILITY TO FAIL FORWARD

This is a fun quality to have with your team/organization. You are and can be a lifelong learner. Contrary to trendy belief, leaders do not have all the answers—so express yourself with vulnerability and an open-minded. Share with your team that failure is *not* the final word. Doing so is a terrific opportunity to discuss skill development and any additional information that may be implemented. It is the gateway for you as the heart-centered leader, showing that you can move on from failure and into success.

"Nurturing determination and perseverance is the only way to fail forward and accomplish your goals."

Are you demonstrating that you are a leader who always offers to see failure as a learning moment?

Are you able to consistently demonstrate your ability to ensure failure has its place in personal and professional development?

Is your organizational culture founded on failure-as-a-learning moment for advancement?

To appreciate the role empathy plays in leadership, we first need to have a clear understanding of what it means. Most times, we tend to confuse empathy with sympathy; we assume being empathetic means agreeing with or relating to the feelings another person has regarding a given situation or individual.

However, empathy relates more to understanding the needs of others. It means that you are aware of how they're feeling and how it impacts their perception. It doesn't mean you have to agree with how they see things; rather, it shows that you're willing and able to appreciate what the other person is going through. This calls for a repeat visit for the leader to sit in the observer's chair and hone the ability to intrinsically validate the other person. It is in great alignment with Commitment.

"A leader's capacity for empathy is the single most important factor in determining the success of the team. It's what gets people to trust others, to believe in what they're saying, and to commit to following them."

Are you demonstrating that you are an empathetic leader?

Are you able to consistently demonstrate your ability to be empathetic?

Is your organizational culture founded on empathy?

Heart-Centered Leadership

STRIVE TO MENTOR

©2021 BY DEB CROWE

Leadership is a more formal role within an organization; there is a definite hierarchical difference between a leader and their juniors. Discussions between leaders and juniors are likely to relate to professional matters such as assignment progress or questions to clarify instructions.

In contrast, mentorship is more casual. The mentee is likely to feel freer about approaching their mentor about personal and professional issues alike. In this way, the casual nature of the mentor-mentee relationship is more holistic, addressing a wider range of abilities to develop for the mentee. When you can balance being both a leader *and* mentor, it is a clear demonstration of Servant Leadership and also aligns with Approachable and Trustworthy.

"A mentor is someone who allows you to awaken the voice inside yourself."

Are you demonstrating that you are a leader who always strives to mentor?

Are you able to consistently demonstrate your ability to be a mentor?

Is your organizational culture founded on mentoring?

WHERE DO YOU GO FROM HERE?

Now that you have read the twenty heart-centered leadership qualities and see how they work and integrate, where do you go from here?

Individual and team assessments are a great place to start.

Consider measuring behavior, not personality.

Are you open to learning your metacognition? To a deep dive into deductive reasoning?

You've added a lot to your leadership toolkit here. Allow this to have a great impact on your organization and help your leaders grow.

Now is a great time to have your leaders or team assessed. Email me directly for more information at deb@debcrowe.com.

♥

Leadership is about empathy.

It is about having the ability to relate to
and connect with people for the purpose
of inspiring and empowering their lives.

—OPRAH WINFREY

♥

CHAPTER 9

THE HEART-CENTERED LEADERSHIP MODEL

———

What kind of leadership style is best suited for a heart-centered approach?

How you can lead with your heart while still achieving your goals and objectives?

In 2021, I was asked by our local college to develop a micro-credential leadership series for the business school.

The dean was interested in my perspective of what heart-centered leadership looks from a business perspective.

So, I developed the Heart-Centered Leadership Model (as shown below).

DEBORAH CROWE

HEART-CENTERED LEADERSHIP MODEL

TRANSFORMATIONAL LEADERSHIP

ASSERTIVE LEADERSHIP

MINDFUL LEADERSHIP

INCLUSIVE LEADERSHIP

HEART-CENTERED LEADERSHIP

WWW.DEBCROWE.COM

Heart-centered leadership is the foundation and, indeed, the beginning of every leader's journey.

My definition of heart-centered leadership is honoring your connection with people.

How do we honor our connection with people?

- Attentive listening
- Presence
- Nonverbal communication
- Soft skill exchange
- Avoiding transactional dynamics

How to move to learn and embrace being an inclusive leader is the next step in our heart-centered leadership playbook. My colleague and friend from Australia, Juliet Bourke, co-created the model below (Bourke 2016).

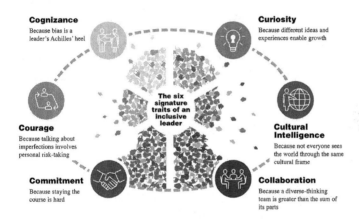

Cognizance
Because bias is a leader's Achilles' heel

Curiosity
Because different ideas and experiences enable growth

Courage
Because talking about imperfections involves personal risk-taking

Cultural Intelligence
Because not everyone sees the world through the same cultural frame

Commitment
Because staying the course is hard

Collaboration
Because a diverse-thinking team is greater than the sum of its parts

The six signature traits of an inclusive leader

Inclusionary leadership is a dedication to the fair treatment of people and ideas. This strategy encourages leaders to recognize their biases and remain open while formulating policies and making choices.

There are many traits leaders must adopt to be more inclusive, and I feel that these qualities are within the heart-centered leadership playbook. Humility, empathy, vulnerability, and resilience are among the most foundational. The journey to becoming an inclusive leader is very personal and offers the opportunity to self-audit one's behavior and increase self-awareness.

Now that you are well equipped to be a heart-centered leader who embraces and models inclusive leadership, it allows the growth to become a mindful leader.

Mindful leadership has also been viewed as lacking in the traditional toolkit. And yet, it is one of the most important facets of leadership, especially when you seek the level of being heart-centered and inclusive.

Mindful leadership is a type in which managers learn how to intentionally build their capacity to be present, open-minded, and compassionate when interacting with their team members—plus they also practice self-care. Once you have mastered mindful leadership, you now can navigate to assertive leadership.

Assertive leadership often gets confused with aggression. Instead, this is a communication style in which individuals confidently and considerately share their opinions, ideas, and expectations with their teams. This form of leadership requires collaboration with individuals at all organizational levels.

Aggression and assertiveness are not synonymous. Communicating assertively demonstrates consideration for the needs of others, but speaking aggressively does not. Be respectful, precise, and firm. This entails actively listening and demonstrating attention or care, especially with heart.

Transformational leadership is the top of the model and represents the C-suite leader level (CEO, COO, CFO, CIO, CTO, CHO, CSO, CMO, CPO, CXO, CHRO, etc.). If previous leadership styles have not been learned, honed, and sustained, this level can significantly affect an organization's culture.

Transformational leadership is an approach that affects individuals and social systems. In its ideal form, it produces beneficial and constructive changes in followers, intending to transform them into leaders.

This model has led to many exciting conversations. When transformational leaders discuss their journey with me, there are elements from my model that they feel are missing or have not experienced. Being a transformational leader is brave. They are different leaders who believes in leading with heart, love, and modeling self-care. In their eyes and belief, it's the only way.

Yet, the world is not opening quickly to the heart-centered leadership model. Some CEOs have told me it's too much "fluff" and needs to be more aligned with the principles of business acumen. I think it belongs in the middle; it's the heart of each business acumen element.

I created the diagram below to align with the principles of business acumen.

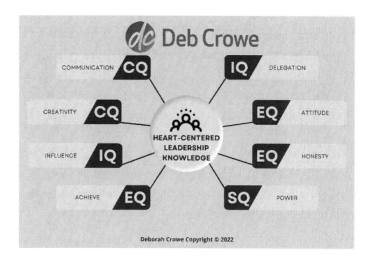

In the Venn diagram below, the intersection of business acumen can achieve heart by modifying and implementing habits from the heart-centered leadership model discussed above. Order is vital to attain heart-centered leadership.

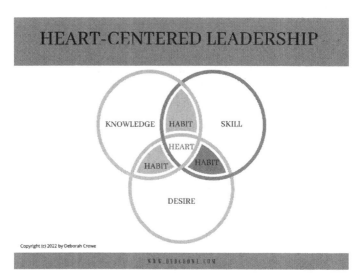

Crowe, Deborah. 2021. The Heart-Centered Leadership Model. Ontario,
CA: Deb Crowe.

The hierarchy of needs is an idea in psychology proposed by American psychologist Abraham Maslow (Maslow 1943).

Maslow's theory emulates what we want and need within heart-centered leadership. We all want to be seen, heard, loved, and validated. It also encompasses what we discuss later in the "Managing the Inner Leader" chapter. It is the foundation to reach the next leader level based on my diagram and leadership series.

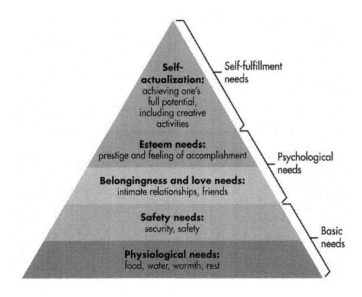

I was so interested and intrigued when I read Dr. Susan David's book, *Emotional Agility*, and reviewed her emotional pyramid of needs (David 2022). Maslow's hierarchy and Dr. David's pyramid are both models that explore human needs and well-being, but they approach the subject from different perspectives.

Here's a comparison of the two models:

CONCEPTUAL BASIS

Maslow's Hierarchy of Needs: Suggests that individuals have a set of hierarchical needs that must be fulfilled in a specific order, starting from basic physiological needs, and progressing to higher-level psychological needs.

Dr. Susan David's Emotional Pyramid of Needs: Focuses on emotional well-being and proposes a framework that emphasizes the importance of emotional agility, adaptability, and mindfulness for a healthy emotional life.

STRUCTURE

Maslow's Hierarchy of Needs: Structured as a pyramid with five levels. The lower levels represent more basic needs, such as physiological needs (food, water, shelter), safety needs (security, stability), and social needs (belonging, love). The higher levels encompass psychological needs (esteem, self-worth) and self-fulfillment needs (self-actualization, personal growth).

Dr. Susan David's Emotional Pyramid of Needs: Also a pyramid, but consisting of three levels. The foundation is labeled "Showing Up" and focuses on being present, aware, and mindful. The middle level is "Stepping Out," which involves emotional agility, adaptability, and resilience. The top level is "Walking Your Talk," which emphasizes aligning actions with values and pursuing meaningful goals.

FOCUS

Maslow's Hierarchy of Needs: Primarily focuses on human motivation and the progression of needs from basic survival to higher-level fulfillment. It addresses a wide range of needs encompassing physical, social, and psychological aspects of human life.

Dr. Susan David's Emotional Pyramid of Needs: Emphasizes emotional well-being, psychological flexibility, and living a values-aligned life. It also focuses on developing emotional intelligence, adaptability, and resilience to navigate life's challenges effectively.

UNIVERSAL VERSUS INDIVIDUAL

Maslow's Hierarchy of Needs: Suggests that the hierarchy of needs is universal and applies to all individuals, regardless of cultural or individual differences. It assumes that everyone has similar needs and motivations.

Dr. Susan David's Emotional Pyramid of Needs: Acknowledges that emotional needs and well-being can vary across individuals and cultures. It recognizes the importance of personal values and individual emotional experiences in shaping our needs.

HISTORICAL CONTEXT

Maslow's Hierarchy of Needs: Developed in the mid-twentieth century and has been influential in various fields, such as psychology, human resources, and education.

Dr. Susan David's Emotional Pyramid of Needs: A more recent development and influenced by contemporary research on emotions, mindfulness, and well-being.

While both models explore human needs and well-being, they differ in their specific focus, structure, and underlying assumptions. Both models, though, can provide valuable insights into understanding and enhancing human experiences.

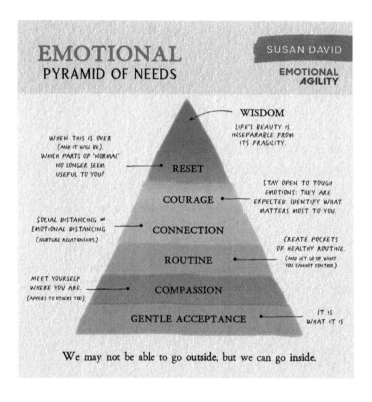

David, Susan. 2022. "Emotional Pyramid of Needs." Susan David (blog).
October 12, 2022.
https://www.susandavid.com/resource/emotional-pyramid-of-needs.

One of the most important conversations I have with leaders at all levels is about the ability to embrace imperfection. I always ask two specific questions:

1. Is there room in your leadership for imperfection?
2. Can you offer the ability to model failing forward?

This is a great starting point for the leader to audit their introspection. I firmly believe you cannot achieve transformational leadership without starting from the bottom and learning to master the art of heart, which is genuinely heart-centered leadership. My opinion stems from fourteen years as an executive leadership and life coach and repeatedly hearing from all levels of leadership that they don't have or never learned how to be heart-centered.

The other challenge is that many organizations do not have a coaching culture.

It's easy to assign a title or stature to a leader.

It's hard to ensure they are ready, willing, and able. And most leaders fear to claim the three fearful words—"I don't know"—about a task or their own skill set.

Where do we go from here?

Here are some steps to help you effectively integrate new leadership information and tools:

1. Stay curious: Develop a mindset of continuous curiosity. Stay updated with the latest trends, research, and insights in the field of heart-centered leadership. Follow reputable sources, read books, and engage in discussions with other leaders through workshops, seminars, and conferences.

2. Evaluate relevance: When you come across new heart-centered leadership information or tools, assess their relevance to your specific context and goals. Consider the needs of your team, organization, and industry. Not all information and tools will apply to your situation, so focus on those that do.

3. Research and verify: Before incorporating any new information or tools, conduct thorough research to verify credibility and effectiveness. Look for evidence-based practices and seek input from trusted experts or mentors who have experience with the concepts or tools you're considering.

4. Begin with baby steps: Implement new information and tools gradually, rather than trying to overhaul your entire leadership approach overnight. Start with small, manageable changes that align with your current practices. Experiment with new ideas and observe their impact before expanding their use.

5. Integrate with existing frameworks: Find ways to mesh new information and tools with your existing heart-centered leadership framework. Identify commonalities and connections between what you already know and the new concepts. This integration will help you create a coherent and consistent approach.

6. Collaborate and share: Share your insights, exchange ideas, and learn from others' experiences. Collaborative learning with other leaders can enhance the implementation process and create a supportive environment for growth.

7. Reflect and adapt: Regularly think back on your experiences and outcomes after incorporating new information and tools. Assess their effectiveness, gather

feedback from your team, and be open to adjusting. Adaptation is crucial for refining your leadership approach and maximizing its impact.

8. Develop a group learning culture: Foster a culture of continuous learning within your team or organization. Encourage everyone to explore new heart-centered leadership resources, attend relevant training programs, and share their insights with others. By creating a team learning culture, you can collectively benefit.

FULL-CIRCLE LIFE MOMENT:
Remember—heart-centered leadership is a journey, and the process of incorporating new information and tools is ongoing. Embrace the opportunity to grow and evolve as a leader daily and be open to refining your practices based on new insights and experiences.

♥

Find a way to work with people;
it will change your life.

—DAVID MARTIN

♥

CHAPTER 10

BUSINESS ACUMEN WITH HEART

How can you combine your business acumen with heart-centered leadership to create a thriving and compassionate workplace?

The intersection of business strategy and heart-centered leadership is where you can leverage both to achieve sustainable success.

From leveraging diversity and inclusion to building trust and fostering innovation, this chapter provides practical tips and insights for creating a business culture that is not only profitable but also fulfilling and empowering for everyone involved.

Leadership has always leaned on the foundation and principles of a basic playbook: knowledge, skill, and ability.

But there is no heart-centered leadership playbook. I scratch my head and wonder why.

Over the years after starting my company, I was told the words "heart" and "love" do not belong in leadership language or business acumen.

The capacity to comprehend business concerns is known as acumen. It is the accumulation of information on how and why things are done on general and organization-specific levels. It is a crucial quality for leadership, manifesting in both the queries someone poses and the choices they make. When I look at its definition, I wonder how leaders (people) can lead with greatness for an organization (also people) that is without heart.

I believe we lost heart-centered leadership at the start of the Industrial Revolution. The opportunity of business, sales, and the almighty dollar became apparent: the juncture where ego grows and money is made.

Don't get me wrong; I am an entrepreneur and I provide a service, charge a fee, and get paid. My point is that when we follow the principles of heart-centered leadership and adopt a people-over-profit mentality, the money comes without the ego ever being involved.

Before I started my company, I was told I was too nice, too giving, too gregarious, too kind, and that I laughed too much—my first real exposure to leadership and leaders without heart.

Fast forward thirty-three years, and here we are. The world is slowly emerging from the other side of a global pandemic.

Work shows up in our life. Life shows up in our work. We need a common ground to connect—that is, to lead with our hearts.

As we continue to navigate unprecedented times in a heavy world, we need heart-centered leadership.

One of my favorite heart-centered leaders is Mike Sievert of T-Mobile. Prior to the role, he was COO and mentored by CEO John Legere to take over when he retired.

This story intrigued me at the human level. John used his transformational leadership skills to prepare Mike for his transition from COO to CEO. John saw something in Mike and helped him take on the role. Seems simple and brilliant at the same time—yet it takes a heart-centered, visionary leader to create the time and space for a leadership undertaking at this level.

In 2022, Mike was named CNN Business CEO of the Year, a high level of recognition at the C-suite level (La Monica 2022).

I wanted Mike to have a place in my heart-centered leadership playbook because, as a leader, he cares. When we feel nervous deciding in life or leadership, it's because we care about the people involved.

Here is an example of Mike's heart-centered leadership:

"I am still learning. This quote has been attributed—and misattributed—to so many thinkers throughout the centuries that, at this point, it sounds generic. Whether it was Michelangelo, Ralph Waldo Emerson, Norman Rockwell, or someone else, the words express a simple yet powerful idea: Even the masters never stop growing.

"The contemporary term for this openness to new ideas is growth mindset. As a theory of intelligence, the growth mindset is one in which our interests, skills, and aptitudes can develop over time. And hey, there's science behind it. Studies show that when a company embraces a growth mindset, it can go a long way toward improving employee diversity, mental health, job satisfaction, and performance.

"During my first full year as CEO, my goal has been to embrace a growth mindset – to continue being proactive about learning and constantly improving, for myself and for T-Mobile. To that end, I've been looking at the ways successful leaders do their thing and infusing some of the resulting ideas into how I lead this company...

"I encourage my leaders at T-Mobile to listen and consider all perspectives. But ultimately, we are all responsible for our own decisions. You can't let pressure from someone else stand in the way of making the choices you need to make (for me, being what's best for our customers, employees, and shareholders). My leadership team and I approach tough decision-making with General Powell's advice in mind: Get enough information to make an informed decision, and then trust your gut. Also, be willing to learn and grow from your mistakes.

"I'm happy to take notes from such strong, empathetic individuals. This is all about embracing an optimistic view of the future – one that's wide open *to possibility. And when we keep learning, we keep improving. That's what the growth mindset is all about. Because as good as we are, I know we can get even better. And that pursuit is what moves me and my teammates at T-Mobile" (Sievert 2021).*

Mike recently celebrated his tenth "Magentaversary" at T-Mobile, and I really enjoyed reading his reflection:

"When I joined Team Magenta, T-Mobile was rebuilding from a failed merger but working on another with MetroPCS. We didn't yet offer the iPhone, or LTE service. We were focused on prepaid and our 'challenger strategy' in urban areas and just starting to firm up plans for a new groundbreaking Un-carrier approach that would change wireless as we knew it. That's just scratching the surface, but yep, A LOT has happened in that time." (Sievert 2022)

Here are Mike's top ten takeaways:

1. Smart risks lead to rewards
2. Competition fuels innovation
3. Don't be afraid to swim upstream
4. Create a culture that includes everyone
5. Never stop learning and growing
6. Success creates success
7. Mistakes uncover fresh thinking
8. It's better to be an owner
9. We can use our platform to generate real impact
10. Perseverance is a virtue—if you are right

I had the honor to present to Mike and his leadership team on a panel in January 2022. They created a one-day, heart-leadership-themed summit, and I was their lunch keynote speaker.

I shared my presentation in a written booklet afterward, as Mike loved what I presented and said his leaders couldn't write fast enough during my presentation. Caring matters.

I left the leaders of T-Mobile with my recipe for success in leading with heart:

DEB CROWE'S HEART-CENTERED RECIPE

INGREDIENTS

- Patience
- Heart
- Love
- Generosity
- Understanding
- Laughter
- Loyalty
- Kindness

PROCEDURE

01 Take two heaping cups of patience, one heartful of love and two handfuls of generosity.

02 Mix well and sprinkle generously with kindness.

03 Spread this irresistible delicacy over a lifetime and serve everybody you meet.

PREP TIME

- Prep|Daily
- Ready|Always ready to serve
- Duration|A lifetime

FULL-CIRCLE LIFE MOMENT:

Every leader wants to succeed regardless of their title, role, level of responsibility, or sector. Some choose their leadership as their full-time role and allow it to take over their life and health. Others find a delicate way to balance it and demonstrate the beauty of being heart-centered.

♥

As we look ahead into the next century,
leaders will be those who empower others.

—BILL GATES

♥

CHAPTER 11

THE SELF-CARE JOURNEY IN LEADERSHIP

——

Have you ever sensed that you are becoming who you are meant to be?

That is how I felt when I turned thirty. I was also twenty weeks pregnant and still did not know. Tired and feeling nauseated, I thought I had the flu. I had been married for three years—a wonderful, joyous, exciting time in my life. Then, on February 14, 1995, my husband and I learned we were having our first baby, and we were so excited!

Sadly, we lost our baby boy one week later.

The doctors couldn't tell us why this happened, and my emptiness and sadness were gut-wrenching. Turning to my faith again, I lay on the couch for a week crying for our baby and asking God why he had done this. I needed a reprieve from unbearable loss, sadness, and trauma.

Five months later, we learned that we were expecting again!

John and I welcomed a baby girl (Christine) in January 1996 and were further blessed with another baby girl (Laura) in October 1997.

Still, I continued to face more loss and grief when my oldest brother, Jim, died of cancer at forty-three in December 1999. I was emotionally unable to visit him and could not cope with his declining health. The situation brought me back to age twenty-one and felt like I was with my dad again—a grief-trigger moment.

Perhaps reopening that pain and grief—those trigger memories— created post-traumatic flashbacks. In any case, I was unable to be fully present for him. My sister-in-law ridiculed me and did not permit me to visit him at home or attend his funeral.

It's hard to grieve when you aren't allowed to say goodbye.

I share this with you here in the heart-centered leadership playbook because all life moments—good, bad, or neutral—have a purpose. We are given barriers, obstacles, and challenges so we can show up and be the leader of our life. Sometimes it's hard. I guess I've never had the opportunity to sit or wallow (an expression from my Irish Nana).

Life continued to progress forward—and fast. I felt rushed again, burdened with schedules and deadlines. I felt the pressure of having to be the perfect Supermom, trying to be Betty Crocker and Martha Stewart, all while building my business as an entrepreneur and traveling extensively.

There were days and weeks when I didn't have time to take a break. And when we stay busy, we don't have time to think or feel. I needed to get off life's treadmill and not repeat... repeat... repeat...

In moments of doubt, I turn to my faith to rediscover my determination and reassure myself that I am indeed a good person. My feelings matter. I continued to grow and learn and returned to university, embracing my love for neuroscience and the brain—specifically brain injury.

The midlife wisdom I've gained now is that sometimes on our life journey, we must stand up for ourselves even when it's emotionally painful. People (including family) will leave our lives.

But sometimes we must let things be, as they are no longer in our control. Accept. Let it go. Move on.

We cannot live running on an empty tank. Self-care and nurturing is the key to longevity. Growth can sometimes be very lonely, but that's fine because you enjoy your company and know who you are. The observation alone is priceless.

I made time (a.k.a., white space) appear in my schedule: one hour daily. I needed to pour into myself to be a better wife and mother. One hour each day for self-care is not only required, but also necessary.

Self-care is not as elusive as it once was. Luckily, it's becoming widely accepted as a staple of healthy living. Taking time for ourselves, whether with yoga, meditation, fitness, or even a long, relaxing bath, will help us get through the day and keep us healthy long-term.

Nevertheless, many people are still out there—hard-working moms, workaholics, diligent students, you name it—who see self-care as indulgent and over-permissive. They don't feel deserving or feel like they're slacking off when not working until near exhaustion.

The fact of the matter is: Giving ourselves time to unwind and relax is healthy and necessary, and it needn't be time-consuming.

WHAT IS SELF-CARE?

Self-care can take on many shapes and sizes and is unique to everyone. It is anything and everything that makes us feel happy, confident, and whole. Yoga, light physical exercises, showering, traveling, reading, clothes shopping, listening to music, or meditating are, among many others, some examples of self-care.

The beauty here is that the more we care for ourselves, the better and brighter our days become. If done regularly, we won't want or need to change a thing. And, as luck would have it, the only person standing in the way of investing more time in ourselves—is us!

ELIMINATE DISTRACTIONS AND TIME WASTERS

Far too many people don't take the necessary time for themselves because they feel they don't have enough time to begin with. And, unbeknownst to us, plenty of time-wasters and distractions still eat up a lot of our work time.

Stop checking your emails regularly. Stop multitasking. Delegate more. Start saying *no* from time to time. Keep yourself organized. Stop creating interruptions like sending texts to friends while at work. These are a few examples of what you can do to save time. When you do, you'll be surprised to see how much of our energy we waste on trivial things.

ESTABLISH A ROUTINE

As with any habit, becoming and keeping yourself motivated is hard. There is no one-size-fits-all approach to the issue, but it is best to begin with the moment you arise in the morning. Wake up gently and happily, and don't rush anything—this way, you'll be sufficiently energized to start your day correctly.

Don't be too hard on yourself. Self-care shouldn't be seen as a chore; it is quite the opposite. Make it an effortless experience by preparing your space ahead of time. Don't let yourself be tempted to check your emails or social media.

Last, you must give yourself enough time to complete the routine without rushing. Initially, you may feel you've wasted precious time by taking some for yourself—but don't give in to that apprehension.

I suggest you start with twenty minutes of self-care daily, then move to thirty to sixty minutes as you become more comfortable. You can even spread this time throughout the day into three twenty-minute periods: one in the morning, one at lunch, and another in the evening. Altogether, this is only 4 percent of the day that you've dedicated solely to yourself. That doesn't sound like much!

Selfishness and selflessness are two sides of the same coin. As the ancient Taoist religion of China teaches us, there is no such thing as something outstanding or terrible. There cannot be darkness without light, as there cannot be heat without cold. The same thing holds for selfishness and selflessness.

Every person who has ever lived has been both selfish *and* selfless at the same time. Some of us may be selfish with our material possessions, while others may be selfish when sharing feelings or opening to others. In today's world, it only stands to reason that no utterly selfless person could ever survive. People would take advantage until there was nothing else left to give.

This doesn't mean we should be entirely selfish either because, in a sense, we would end up in the same place. We need *both* to survive and make the world a better place. When it comes to survival, selfishness is vital—but selflessness is crucial when talking about our personal lives.

Being emotionally selfish with loved ones will almost always lead to a breakup in relationships. Unfortunately, it can be difficult to regulate our selfish behavior. Nevertheless, it is only through those selfish instincts that we can hope to understand and embody selflessness.

DOES MODELING SELF-CARE AS A HEART-CENTERED LEADER HELP YOUR DIRECT TEAM AND ORGANIZATION AS A WHOLE?

Some research through the National Institute of Health supports "yes" in answer to this question (Martínez et al 2021). Of course, leadership plays an important role in employee well-being. But, despite growing academic interest in leaders' resources as determinants of healthy leadership, it is not yet clear how behavior regarding their own health (i.e., self-care) may trickle down to employees.

Drawing on the Conservation of Resources Theory and the model of Health-Oriented Leadership, this study tests two mechanisms through which employees may benefit from self-caring leaders: (a) through staff care, that is, concern for their employees' health (improved leadership hypothesis); and (b) through a direct relationship between leaders' and employees' self-care (role-modeling hypothesis). In turn, both staff care and employee self-care would relate positively to employee health. Multilevel path models based on a sample of $N = 46$ supervisors and 437 employees revealed that leader self-care was positively related to leader-rated staff care at Level 2, which was positively related to employee-rated staff care at Level 1. In turn, employee-rated staff care was positively related to employee health.

The findings support the improved leadership hypothesis and underline the importance of leader self-care as a determinant of healthy leadership. (Klug 2022).

As a heart-centered leader, I have witnessed this firsthand. In one instance, I had one staff member with breast cancer and another with a child who had a developmental disability. Both women were fatigued, exhausted, uncertain, and laden with guilt and worry for the future. I leaned in with my heart to listen and be present. Then I worked with them to discover solutions and strategies and find individual plans for their families. I also modeled self-care by regularly taking time off for my own mental health and well-being.

THE ROAD TO SELFLESSNESS IS THROUGH SELFISHNESS

As we've established, selfishness and selflessness are intertwined—not mutually exclusive. Selfishness will help us thrive economically, while selflessness helps us in our social endeavors.

But since material desires and necessities sit at the bottom of Maslow's Hierarchy of Needs, it would stand to reason that selfishness is more ingrained and harder to control. Nevertheless, as we go up this pyramid of needs, selflessness becomes the prime ingredient for success. Love, belonging, self-esteem, and self-actualization can never be achieved without being selfless.

If we boil it down, selflessness is about giving up something for someone else's benefit. It can be hard to find any reason to be selfless when we know what we want and how we want it—that is, until we find ourselves on the receiving end of selfishness.

During these times, we learn selflessness. In fact, doing so wouldn't be possible without knowing selfishness firsthand, both as a user and a receiver.

Likewise, we've all been in a situation where we want to move our personal space away from scrutiny. This means that we are actively looking to keep secrets—to feel that nobody has their eyes and ears on us. This search for independence has made us all push away our parents, siblings, or partners at some point.

But as necessary as this "breathing space" is, we should never go as far as excluding our loved ones from our lives for it. If things are unchecked, we risk building an insurmountable emotional wall.

By choice, solitude is excellent. But when we continuously distance ourselves from the closest people in our lives, we will find ourselves utterly alone in a time of need and things will inevitably be more difficult.

It is, thus, through selfishness that we develop the necessary empathy to discover selflessness.

FULL-CIRCLE LIFE MOMENT

It's truly the little things that make life beautiful, and self-care is an expression of that. Don't be afraid of being happy and whole; otherwise, you'll regret it.

♥

I fell into leadership
as I used my heart first.

—STEVE MACCLURE

♥

CHAPTER 12

FORGIVENESS IN LEADERSHIP

———

How can forgiveness transform our lives and become a powerful tool for heart-centered leadership?

Well, for one, it can help us overcome setbacks to move forward with compassion and resilience.

Forgiveness can become a cornerstone of your leadership approach and can help you create a more compassionate and supportive work environment.

This is not an easy topic for most people, including myself. I have had a tremendous amount of loss in this life. I lost my dad when I was twenty-one and now, at fifty-seven, I'm realizing how young *he* was when he passed away.

I was too young to have had so many of his caregiving responsibilities placed on my shoulders—but the rest of my family abandoned this role. Responsibility gave me my love for medical information, rehabilitation, and the gift of whole-heartedly being there without judgment, only love.

As you know, my mother was not maternal and, therefore, didn't show or give love on a regular basis. She did the best she could with the education she had and the tools she picked up along the way. Still, she struggled with deep-seated grief, depression, anxiety, and alcoholism, and, as a result, became abusive.

Since 1987, I have been in survival mode. Fight-or-flight was my normal.

Then, on top of all that pain, my Nana died nine months before my wedding. I felt devastated and heartbroken—I hadn't been able to even see her to say goodbye.

I share my losses with you to show that, as human beings, we share many things in common. We've dealt with the same challenges, especially if you too have suffered from loss.

There are life situations in which we see the value of loss, grief, and a broken heart. It's not the pain or loss that was my focus. I tried to navigate the story, the timeline—and, yes, it brought me to my knees. But the beauty of it is that I got up from the floor, healed, and enjoyed the results of these life experiences.

We all have loss and trauma in our lives. But it's not what happens to us; it's how we choose to respond. I chose to forgive my parents, my brother, and Nana for leaving me. To top things off, I also forgave my mother for everything else—because I truly believe she loved me in the best way she could, with what she was taught.

My point is that we must take the time we need to heal and undergo the stages of complicated grief. When we're ready, and when it feels right, we can take the next step in the right direction and forgive.

Forgiveness to me is the surrendering of emotional thought and feeling. We release ourselves from emotional overdraft, then allow enough space to take a deep breath and inhale the goodness for ourselves. We feel free for the first time.

Using a chart like the one below is a good way to start listing things that bother you. In turn, this allows you to become present and seek forgiveness.

Situation or incident:	Emotion you feel/felt:	Who would you like to forgive?

When working with leaders, I have observed many different behavioral outcomes. My favorite line on the topic? "Life shows up at work, and work shows up in life."

When we can embrace our self-awareness and allow room for mistakes and imperfection, it makes us more relatable to each other as human beings.

Listening is a key strategy to forgiveness. We give our whole selves to that other person. We hear them. We see them. We feel them. We validate them. The beauty of this strategy is that we don't even have to speak. We are physically present. Our energy can be felt by others.

Nonverbal communication is powerful.

Albert Mehrabian, a researcher specializing in body language, was the first to break down the components of face-to-face conversation. He found that communication is 55 percent nonverbal, 38 percent vocal, and 7 percent words-only (The University of Texas Permian Basin 2023).

Our thought habits play a huge role in forgiveness. When we can mentally leave room to be present, it helps us understand what we said or what has been said to us. In doing so, we allow logic to be the forerunner of our thoughts. Logic takes the lead, and emotional resilience allows us to be seen, heard, and validated.

Forgiveness, in my humble opinion, is a superpower. It demonstrates that we can be a leader who understands and allows the space for everyone to show up—however they need to. This is not meant to be taken as an obligation. Rather, it's meant to share with you that we all have the power to live our lives through self-direction. We have the power to affirm what we want and how we want it.

Forgiving someone within the workplace can be a powerful and transformative act that not only benefits the individual involved but also fosters a healthier and more productive work environment. To begin the process of forgiveness, it's essential to first understand your own emotions surrounding the situation.

Take time to reflect on the impact the incident has had on you; try to recognize any resentment or anger you may be holding onto. Once you have gained clarity, consider the other person's perspective. Empathy plays a crucial role in forgiving others—allowing you to understand the possible intentions, motivations, and external factors that contributed to their actions.

Engage in open and honest communication with the person involved and express your feelings and concerns while actively listening to their perspective. This dialogue can provide an opportunity for mutual understanding and a chance to rebuild trust.

Commit to letting go of the past and embracing a mindset of forgiveness. Remember that this doesn't mean condoning bad behavior or forgetting the incident, but rather releasing the negative emotions to allow yourself a sense of freedom and peace moving forward.

By practicing forgiveness within the workplace, you create a culture of compassion, empathy, and growth—enabling all kinds of relationships to thrive.

Our thoughts are powerful. Our language is even more powerful. When we combine and align our thoughts and language, we can be the best version of ourselves.

As a heart-centered leader, if our actions are not aligned, it can reveal how easily our ego can come into play, leading to a systematic approach influenced by our ego.

When we become black-and-white in our thoughts and language, how does that leave space for anyone else to feel confident approaching us with an uncomfortable topic?

Forgiveness is an important aspect of heart-centered leadership. It can help build strong relationships, foster understanding, and create a more positive work environment. When leaders make mistakes, they can show their employees that they're not perfect—that they're willing to take responsibility and apologize.

Additionally, when leaders forgive their team members, it can help create an atmosphere of respect and mutual understanding. It can also help foster a sense of collaboration and creativity within the team. Ultimately, forgiveness at the leadership level can be a powerful tool for creating a successful and productive work environment.

Forgiveness can also be a powerful tool on a psychological level, helping us to move away from negative emotions such as anger, resentment, and bitterness and, instead, focus on positive emotions such as empathy, understanding, and acceptance. It can help us develop a healthier relationship with ourselves, allowing us to better cope with stressful situations and learn from our mistakes.

Ultimately, forgiveness can bring us a greater sense of inner peace, contentment, and well-being—all heart-centered qualities.

FULL-CIRCLE LIFE MOMENT:
Our greatest losses can be beautiful learning moments that leave us better, whole, happy, and heart-centered.

♥

To the heart in you,
don't be afraid to feel.

To the sun in you,
don't be afraid to shine.

To the love in you,
don't be afraid to heal.

—NAJWA ZEBIAN

♥

CHAPTER 13

THE VALUE OF INTUITION MANAGEMENT

———

How can we cultivate and trust our intuition as a valuable heart-centered leadership tool?

Let's explore the power of intuition in decision-making and how you can learn to tune in to your inner guidance to make better choices and lead with authenticity and purpose. This chapter provides practical tips and exercises for developing your intuition and building trust in your instincts.

Intuition management has been a topic of interest for me since starting my company in 1990. Because I was only twenty-four years young, intuition always played a big part in my life for many decisions.

A great example of intuition is when we are in an environment where "something" doesn't feel right. It makes us feel, think, and conclude that something is displaced.

Another example is when I facilitate groups of people. We can easily observe nonverbal communication around us. Energy is everywhere. We can see and *feel* the uneasiness when we tap into our intuition. The gift of using intuition management is noticing everything and everyone around us. I've witnessed this personally and professionally with people across all different sectors.

It's a skill, when mastered, that offers an opportunity to observe, learn, practice, and integrate its use into our lives. It's an invitation to further augment and master the art of heart in life and leadership.

C-suite leaders have long challenged me about intuition management. It's only later, after heart-level conversations, that their disbelief dissipates. When we have honest, safe conversations, intuition is the foundation of our self-awareness and belief systems.

INTUITION IN BUSINESS MANAGEMENT

Intuition in business management is an innovative means of utilizing your innate senses to help guide decision-making. Most often, it relies on a business leader's gut feeling and experience to make the best choices for the company.

This management style can lead to greater productivity and creativity within the workplace, as it encourages employees to think outside the box and consider alternative solutions. It also demonstrates each team member's unique strengths and weaknesses, allowing for a more collaborative approach to problem-solving.

Ultimately, intuition business management provides a unique and effective way for companies to succeed in today's competitive landscape.

THE SIXTH SENSES

Intuition is certainly a kind of sixth sense for humans; our own instinctive knowledge provides us with a hunch about a person or thing.

Proprioception, another underappreciated "sixth sense," permits us to track where our body parts are in space. When I was a neurotrauma medical case manager, learning about this sense was an "aha moment"; I had witnessed my clients, some of whom sustained traumatic brain or spinal cord injuries, master their sixth sense.

Proprioception is something many of us mistake for intuition. But in the end, it's just limb receptors sensing movement—like muscle spindles and joint receptors that relay information to the brain via neurons. Examples of proprioception include being able to walk or kick without looking at our feet or being able to touch our noses with our eyes closed.

INTUITIONAL BELIEFS

Intuitional beliefs are those based on instinct rather than reason or logic. They are often based on personal experiences and considered reliable sources of knowledge. These beliefs can help us make decisions by providing an individual with an internal sense of right or wrong to guide through times of uncertainty.

If we look at the period from March 2020 to the present day, we have witnessed much intuitional belief unfold. Throughout the pandemic, leaders worldwide have used their intuition to assess their next strategy considering the global crisis. Each country and its leadership determined what they thought would be the best methods to facilitate, manage, and sustain their populations in uncertain times.

At the beginning of the COVID-19 outbreak, there were no files to review, no resources to refer to, nor anyone to ask questions to; it wasn't any kind of crisis we'd experienced in a long, long time.

When I spoke with older adults about the pandemic, their views were interesting. Through the crisis, their intuition aligned with decades of rich experience in life and work. I spoke with individuals in their seventies, eighties, nineties, and beyond. It is genuinely exciting to know we now live longer. These people alluded to the beginning of their lives—how they survived polio, war, the Great Depression, diphtheria, and tuberculosis, to name a few.

My great-grandmother, Alice, had exceptional intuition, and I regret not having had the opportunity to meet her. She gave birth to a son (Jack) and a daughter (Elizabeth, my Irish Nana). Her son contracted diphtheria in England in the early 1900s. With her husband (my great-grandfather, David) at war during this time, she could not find any assistance.

Unfortunately, her son died of his illness. At the same time, her daughter had contracted polio in her right leg, and doctors wanted to amputate it immediately. But a mother's intuition in life and leadership is always present. Alice showed remarkable courage in her decision-making. She buried her son in her backyard, then decided to sail from England to Canada with her daughter.

After the voyage, Canadian doctors advised her they could save Nana's leg. The miraculous outcome came after several surgeries and antibiotic treatment.

I commend my great-grandmother for her intuition and decision-making. As a mother, I can't fathom losing a child then packing up and moving across the ocean to save my other child. Grit, logic, and determination combined with her strong intuition to achieve these triumphs.

Of course, intuition management can be a powerful tool for heart-centered leaders to tap into, too. It can help them make better decisions and connect more deeply with their team members.

To use intuition management in leadership, start by understanding its power. It can offer insights not found through traditional methods. It can also provide valuable information about a team's dynamics and how to better motivate and engage employees.

Once you understand the power of intuition, practice deliberately listening to it. Take the time to pay attention to your instincts and the signals you get from others.

Developing a system to use intuition management in decision-making can involve talking to team members, conducting an in-depth analysis of the issue, then relying on your intuition to make the final call. With practice, intuition management can become an invaluable tool in your leadership toolbox.

THE PRESENCE OF INTUITION MANAGEMENT

Intuition management typically presents when a person has developed a strong self-awareness and is open to exploring and utilizing their inner wisdom. It is often used to help make decisions, evaluate situations, and solve complex problems. It can be helpful in everyday life, providing guidance and clarity through uncertainty.

DEVELOPING TRUST WITH OUR INTUITION

One way to learn to trust your intuition is to practice mindful meditation. This can help you become more aware of inner thoughts, feelings, and emotions—which can, in turn, help you better understand what your intuition is saying.

You can become more aware of any potential obstacles standing in the way: Think back to when you followed your intuition and how the outcome played out. Recognize when your intuition is guiding you in the right direction. Make sure to trust yourself.

Intuition comes from within, so if it feels right, it probably is!

THE LEADER'S INTUITION TOOLKIT

Developing strong leadership skills can be beneficial in managing intuition. It is essential to be able to recognize and trust your gut feelings and be able to make decisions based on it. Having a solid sense of self-awareness and being able to identify critical patterns in different situations can help with intuition management.

Additionally, good communication and problem-solving skills can help understand different perspectives and approaches to a situation, which can then help inform the decision-making process. Strong organizational skills can help you keep track of other ideas and solutions that come up, so you can prioritize the most appropriate ones.

INTUITION MANAGEMENT VERSUS INFORMED INTUITION

Intuition management and informed intuition are two concepts that can help decision-making in various situations.

Intuition management involves using facts, data, and other information to make intuition-based decisions, while informed intuition relies on intuition while considering information.

Both approaches can be practical, depending on the situation and the individual's preferences. Ultimately, it's essential to consider both options and find the best strategy for you, your team, and the organization.

THE BRAIN-GUT CONNECTION

Our brain and gut have an incredibly close connection—one that impacts our thinking. Research from the National

Institutes of Health has shown that the two organs are linked via the gut-brain axis (GBA), a bi-directional communication system. This connection allows our gut to influence our thinking, emotions, and behavior.

For example, if we feel anxious our gut might respond with increased acidity and inflammation, which can interfere with cognitive function. On the other hand, when we feel relaxed and in a positive mental state, our gut will be less inflamed—and our brain will be able to think more clearly.

So you can see why taking care of our physical and mental health is vital to get the most out of our thinking abilities.

LOOKING TO THE FUTURE

As a heart-centered leader, utilizing intuition management means leading with empathy, understanding, and decision-making. It means having a plan that focuses on building meaningful relationships with those you lead while striving to create a culture of trust and collaboration.

When a heart-centered leader uses intuition as a decision-making guide, it will ensure self-inquiry to consider the best interests of those they lead. It's a commitment to listening, asking questions, and using intuition to make decisions the best for everyone.

INTUITIVE HEART-CENTERED LEADERS

Vishen Lakhiani is the founder of MindValley, one of the top personal-growth education-tech platforms in the world. Lakhiani left his dream job at Microsoft to follow his intuition. He often shares that tapping into our hearts is the key to hearing the purpose toward which our intuition guides us (Adams 2020).

Reed Hastings, CEO of Netflix, talks about informed intuition a lot. It's one of his primary leadership skills:

"We start with the data... But the final call is always gut. It is called informed intuition...

"The advantage of Netflix at this stage is that we get to make a number of bets in parallel and manage it like a portfolio... It's a simple fact that data science simply isn't sophisticated enough to predict whether a product will be a hit. Ultimately that rests on a bit of faith that we can predict the future of how consumers will react to a new idea.

"In other words, it's difficult to know which idea will be an outlier, something surprising that doesn't fit the trend. At Netflix, with lots of bets, come lots of opportunity for hits" (Ferenstein 2016).

HOW TO FIND YOUR GUT

Instinct can be a complex process, but a few tips can help you along the way.

First, practice mindfulness and meditation, which can help clear your mind and focus on your innermost feelings and thoughts.

Consider keeping a journal in which to write your thoughts and feelings. This can be a helpful way of getting in touch with your intuition.

Take time to reflect on your life experiences, both positive and negative. By looking back, you start to get a better understanding of how your gut instinct guides you forward.

RECOGNIZE YOUR INTUITIVE LEADERS

Intuitive leaders often exhibit vital emotional intelligence, empathy, creativity, and the ability to think outside the box. They may also have a strong sense of purpose and vision and the ability to inspire and motivate others to achieve common goals. Look for people able to trust their instincts and make decisions based on a combination of rational analysis and intuition. Intuitive leaders may be more likely to take risks, embrace change, and respond quickly to emerging opportunities and challenges.

THE ROLE OF CHANCE VERSUS EXPERIENCE

Human beings are exceptional in being able to learn from the experience of others. One of the most essential qualities of a successful, intuitive leader is a breadth of experience from which to draw.

New or less-experienced employees may occasionally make sound decisions due to chance. However, those who have experienced triumphs and disappointments and learned from them are more valuable to your company.

OVERTHINKING VERSUS SHIFTING INTO SECOND GEAR

Those good at displaying intuition can make snap judgments based on their scenario analysis. When their gut tells them to take a specific route, they confidently and swiftly put everything into second gear and get going.

People who don't believe in themselves are more likely to overthink things, second-guess their decisions, and change course, which slows things down.

CONNECTION VERSUS SEPARATION

You may better grasp personality types, interpret body language, predict how others will react, and capitalize on strengths and weaknesses if you're in tune with those around you.

An employee who gets along well with others at work will likely have a natural knack for managing teams and figuring out how best to allocate resources.

They'll also be aware of their limitations and know when to seek external expertise. Those who prefer to isolate themselves will lose touch not only with their intuition and coworkers but also with organizational goals.

AWARE VERSUS IDLE

Knowing the ins and outs of your company's dynamic might help you hone your intuition. Many workers become so caught up in the specifics of their jobs that they forget about everything else going on around them.

An intuitive person can perform their duties admirably *and* step back to look at the company's big picture. Being an intuitive leader is being consciously prepared and ready for changes in business, including the corresponding financial and human resources, as well as other assets.

It's safe to assume that an employee with this level of innate wisdom will have, in the future, a propensity for picking appropriate options while making crucial business decisions.

As you can see, intuition management certainly has its place in a heart-centered leader's toolkit and business acumen.

FULL-CIRCLE LIFE MOMENT:

Sometimes, not all the facts and information are known. This is when we have the chance to tap into our intuition—that inner voice urging us to listen and act, to believe and achieve.

♥

Enlightened leadership is spiritual if we understand spirituality not as some kind of religious dogma or ideology but as the domain of awareness where we experience values like truth, goodness, beauty, love, and compassion, and also intuition, creativity, insight and focused attention.

—DEEPAK CHOPRA

♥

CHAPTER 14

MANAGING THE INNER LEADER

———

How can we manage and cultivate our inner leader to become more effective and heart-centered?

Let's explore the inner landscape of leadership and how you can develop your self-awareness, emotional intelligence, and mindfulness. Here, we'll provide practical tips and exercises for managing stress, building resilience, and connecting with your purpose and values.

Energy management is one of the first elements I address when working with leaders. When we can manage our personal energy effectively and efficiently, it allows for integration of our personal and work lives.

The "management" part is about handling our physical activities, cognitive tasks, and emotional states throughout the day for a happier and healthy life.

According to the diagram below from Loehr and Schwartz, we humans have four different energy sources: the body, emotions, mind, and spirit. Often, people take their energy for granted and do not pay much attention to it. Thankfully, each of these energy sources can be expanded and renewed.

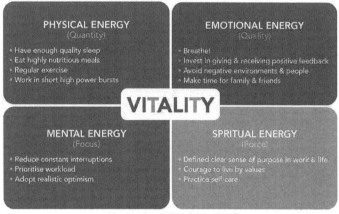

PHYSICAL ENERGY
(Quantity)
• Have enough quality sleep
• Eat highly nutritious meals
• Regular exercise
• Work in short high power bursts

EMOTIONAL ENERGY
(Quality)
• Breathe!
• Invest in giving & receiving positive feedback
• Avoid negative environments & people
• Make time for family & friends

VITALITY

MENTAL ENERGY
(Focus)
• Reduce constant interruptions
• Prioritise workload
• Adopt realistic optimism

SPRITUAL ENERGY
(Force)
• Defined clear sense of purpose in work & life
• Courage to live by values
• Practice self-care

(Adapted from the work of Jim Loehr & Tony Schwartz)

Loehr, Jim and Tony Schwartz. 2004. The Power of Full Engagement.
New York: Simon & Schuster.
https://www.simonandschuster.com/books/
The-Power-of-Full-Engagement/Jim-Loehr/9780743226752.

Writing this chapter brings me back to the conversations I had in 2010 with each of the five executives in hospice care. They had pushed their mental energy so hard that the other levels (physical, emotional, spiritual) led to overdraft. At the end of their lives, they realized, they'd been ignoring all the signs their bodies and minds tried to convey to them.

This chart is vital to help foster, grow, repair, or sustain a culture within organizations. Energy management is for everyone. It's not determined by stature, title, or salary. When every human being can appreciate, integrate, and practice this modality to be and feel, it contributes to a healthy workplace. Happy people mean a happy company.

Leaders who have adapted to efficient levels of energy management are exceptional at mindful leadership. With mindful leadership, managers learn to intentionally build their capacity to be present, open-minded, and compassionate while interacting with their team members—and they extend the same care and regard to themselves.

Energy management has opened the bandwidth on leadership language. When we utilize mindful leadership within our own style and share that with our team, the result is a healthy, vital culture rooted a foundation of corporate wellness.

During my time as a case manager, corporate wellness was primarily associated with disability claims. It was riddled with mitigation, burn rate, and how fast I could get an employee back to work. It was a mental track-and-field game—a race. Despite this, I prided myself on taking my time to develop trust and rapport with my clients to understand why and how they landed inside a disability claim. Every story and person were unique and individual.

Corporate wellness today seems to have run ahead to the forefront of leadership. There now exists a preventive inclusion of mental health practices and looking at employees with a holistic, people-focused lens rather than as a ratio or a spreadsheet of numbers. That is refreshing to see, yet I feel we still have a long way to go.

CORPORATE WELLNESS

Perhaps this is a bold statement: self-care has not had much impact when it comes to leadership. From my vantage point based on the leaders I've worked with over three decades, there is reasoning here.

Business acumen does not come with self-care; it's not part of the language. I'm being neither accusatory nor defensive—merely wanting to share my lived observation, especially as a medical rehabilitation case manager and after losing five executives.

These were all stress-related, short-term disability claims, yet the situation was much worse. They were exceedingly stressed, and it led to their demise. They did not make time or space for self-care.

They realized only too late that climbing the ladder to success *does* come with a cost. If we allow work to take over our lives, there is no room for anything else. Success does not have to come with this particular cost. A successful career can be fully integrated with the important things in our lives: our health and our families.

Being at the top is lonely; marriages break down, and relationships suffer. As an executive leadership and life coach and a neurotrauma case manager for people with disabilities, I've seen this happen a lot.

Here is a list of self-care practices, based on my own use and development as a certified yoga teacher. They've been easily implemented into my executive coaching work and team facilitation.

Intention: *Sankalpa* is the Sanskrit word for intention. *San* means "to become one with" and *kalpa* refers to "time" and "subconscious mind." In LifeForce yoga, we use sankalpa to set an intention, to connect with our hearts' deepest desire (Wellons 2023).

Box Breathing: a relaxation technique that involves taking slow, deep breaths while counting to four on each inhale, holding the breath for four counts, exhaling for four counts, then holding the breath for four counts before repeating the cycle. This technique can help reduce anxiety and promote relaxation (Bunch 2021).

Body Scan: a mindfulness technique that involves taking a mental inventory of your body, starting from your toes, and moving up to your head. It can help you become more aware of physical sensations, reduce stress, and promote relaxation.

Flow Writing: a technique where you write continuously without worrying about spelling, grammar, or punctuation. The goal is to let your thoughts flow freely and capture them on paper or screen. It can be a helpful way to overcome writer's block and generate new ideas.

RAIN: a self-care practice that can help you manage difficult emotions. RAIN stands for recognize, allow, investigate, and nurture.

- Recognize: Acknowledge that you're experiencing a difficult emotion.
- Allow: Allow yourself to feel the emotion without judgment or resistance.
- Investigate: Explore the emotion and its physical sensations without trying to change it.
- Nurture: Offer yourself compassion and kindness as you work through the emotion.

By practicing RAIN, you can cultivate a sense of mindfulness and self-compassion, which can help you better navigate challenging situations (Brach 2023).

Affirmations: positive statements that can help individuals overcome negative thoughts and beliefs. They are used to promote self-confidence, motivation, and a positive mindset. Some examples of affirmations include "I am capable of achieving my goals," "I am worthy of love and respect," and "I choose to focus on the positive."

Sound Healing: a form of therapy that uses sound vibrations to promote physical, emotional, and spiritual healing. It typically involves listening to or creating sounds through instruments such as bowls, gongs, and tuning forks. Some people find it a relaxing and effective way to manage stress and improve overall well-being.

Open Awareness: refers to being fully present and mindful while taking care of oneself. This means paying attention to one's physical, emotional, and mental needs in a nonjudgmental way. By practicing open awareness in self-care, individuals can develop a deeper understanding of their own needs.

Rethinking: examining and possibly changing one's approach to taking care of oneself. This might include reassessing what activities and habits truly benefit one's well-being, like setting boundaries, practicing mindfulness and self-compassion, and seeking support when needed.

Manifestation: refers to the act of bringing a desired outcome or result into reality through intentional and deliberate self-care actions. This can include practices such as setting and achieving personal goals, adopting healthy habits, practicing mindfulness and self-reflection, and prioritizing other self-care activities. By manifesting positive outcomes, individuals can improve their overall quality of life.

Self-Compassion: the practice of treating oneself with kindness, care, and understanding—especially during times of difficulty or failure. It involves recognizing and accepting one's imperfections and mistakes without judgment, and extending the same empathy and compassion toward oneself that one would offer to a friend in need. Research suggests that cultivating self-compassion can lead to greater well-being, resilience, and happiness.

Chakras: believed to be energy centers located in the body that correspond to different physical, emotional, and spiritual aspects of our being. There are seven main chakras, each associated with a specific color, element, and mantra. Balancing these chakras can promote physical and emotional health.

Yoga Nidra: or yogic sleep as it is commonly known, is an immensely powerful meditation technique and one of the easiest yoga practices to develop and maintain. While the practitioner rests comfortably in *savasana* (corpse pose), this systematic meditation takes us through the *pancha maya kosha* (five layers of self), leaving us with a sense of wholeness. No longer must we dread spending hours sitting on the floor waiting for liberation (Jeraci 2023).

Gratitude Journal: a tool used to cultivate gratitude and appreciation by regularly writing things you're thankful for, helping shift your focus toward positivity.

Dynamic Breathing: refers to any technique that involves active and intentional control of breath. It can help improve oxygenation, reduce stress and anxiety, and increase energy levels. Examples of dynamic breathing techniques include deep breathing, box breathing, and alternate nostril breathing.

Somatic Centering: a mindfulness technique that involves focusing on physical sensations in the body to help bring awareness to the present moment and promote relaxation.

Ambient Music: a genre that emphasizes tone and atmosphere over traditional musical structure or rhythm. It often incorporates electronic sounds and loops to create a dreamy, relaxing, or otherworldly mood.

Chanting: refers to the act of rhythmically repeating a phrase or sound, often in a religious or spiritual context. It can also be used as a form of meditation or mindfulness practice.

Forest Bathing (also known as *shinrin-yoku*): a practice of immersing oneself in nature and connecting with the natural surroundings to improve overall well-being. It has been shown to reduce stress, lower blood pressure, and improve mood (Almekinder 2021).

Emotional Healing: the process of addressing and resolving emotional wounds or traumas, which can help individuals feel more balanced and at peace. This can involve different approaches such as therapy, meditation, mindfulness, self-care practices, and more. It is a personal journey that can lead to greater self-awareness and self-esteem.

Reiki: a Japanese technique for stress reduction and relaxation that also promotes healing. It is administered by "laying on hands" and is based on the idea that an unseen "life-force energy" flows through us and is what causes us to be alive.

Being Creative: the ability to use your imagination to come up with original and innovative ideas. It's about thinking outside of the box and finding new ways to approach problems or tasks. Some ways to boost creativity include trying new things, taking risks, and embracing your unique perspective.

Pranayama: a breathing technique in yoga that involves controlling the breath to enhance physical and mental well-being (Karode 2020).

Binaural Beats: an auditory illusion perceived when two different pure-tone sine waves are presented to a listener's ears separately but simultaneously, producing a perceived sound that is actually the difference between the two frequencies. Many people use binaural beats as a form of relaxation, meditation, or to improve focus and concentration. However, the scientific evidence supporting their effectiveness is mixed, and they should not be used as a substitute for professional medical treatment (Soulful Soundwaves 2023).

Improve Focus:

Several techniques can help improve focus.

- Minimize distractions by turning off notifications and finding a quiet workspace.
- Break tasks into smaller, more manageable chunks.
- Use the Pomodoro technique, working for twenty-five minutes then taking a five-minute break.
- Prioritize tasks and focus on the most important ones first.
- Try mindfulness techniques, such as deep breathing or meditation, to clear your mind.

Yoga: a physical, mental, and spiritual practice that originated in ancient India. It involves a series of postures, breathing techniques, and meditation.

Mantra: a sacred, repetitive, and often short phrase, word, or sound that is chanted or recited during meditation or spiritual practices. It is used as a tool to focus the mind, promote inner peace, and enhance concentration. Mantras hold spiritual or psychological significance and are believed to have transformative effects on the individual reciting them.

Metta: a term from Buddhism that refers to the practice of loving-kindness meditation. It involves cultivating an attitude of goodwill toward oneself and others.

The Fake Commute: a concept where people simulate the experience of commuting to work despite working from home. This can involve going for a walk, listening to a podcast or music, or engaging in other activities that mimic the routine of a typical morning commute. The idea is to create a mental separation between home and work, which can help with productivity and mental health.

Self-Inquiry: a process of exploring one's own thoughts, feelings, and beliefs to gain insight into one's true nature and enhance personal growth. It involves asking oneself deep and meaningful questions and reflecting on the answers in an honest and non-judgmental manner.

Goal Setting: the process of identifying something you want to achieve and establishing measurable targets and a plan to reach that outcome. It can help you stay focused, motivated, and track progress toward achievement. Effective goal setting involves setting SMART goals: specific, measurable, achievable, relevant, and time-bound.

When I think about corporate wellness in the past—allowing my mind to go back to the early nineties and continue through to 2009—I see a belief system that had a much different definition. Let me explain the context of this through the eyes of a medical-disability-case manager. Traditionally, corporate wellness has had a foundation in risk management. Wellness wasn't part of the prevention; it was the method to return a person to work. It was a business strategy to mitigate risk.

Fast forward to 2023, and corporate wellness has taken on a new definition—one with a more proactive approach.

Companies and organizations at-large now realize that corporate wellness offerings need to be more preventive-based than mitigation-based.

SO, WHAT DOES CORPORATE WELLNESS MEAN?

Corporate wellness is the ability of an employer to sit in the observer's chair with empathy and exercise the grace of benevolence. People don't decide to get stressed one day. Nor do they want to leave work on a short-term disability claim.

HOW DO WE GET TO THE ETIOLOGY OF HOW AND WHY THIS HAPPENS?

If a work culture is toxic and stressful it wears on people day after day, week after week, until finally, it takes its toll.

The transition for me from case manager to leadership coach was not planned. It was serendipitous. Because I was assigned those three vice presidents and two CEOs who went off on short-term disability claims from stress, I was able to leave when they were gone.

Leading up to that, I had individual time with each to sit, listen, and gather information on how and why this had happened to them. I was taken aback when realizing all five executives were parallel and aligned. They all let the stress of their roles and responsibilities take over their lives.

Are we working for things like boats, cars, cottages, financial freedom?

Or are we climbing toward that success because we've allowed identity and stature to be attached to our worth and worthiness?

Do people respect us more because we have a fancy title?

Because we have established stature—like an expensive car or the big corner office—and we get to wear designer suits?

Or have we relinquished respect as we gained more power?

I'm still trying to figure this out, and I've been in business for thirty-three years.

If you get to the level of executive leadership, I firmly believe using your heart-centered power and a grateful heart makes a difference. This level of thinking and action is like a magnet for miracles. If you think you're going to have something and you want to go get it, then we need to look inward.

Emotional intelligence is one thing. Still, if you don't have the emotional resilience to go along with it, it's like buying something you want and never using it.

Leaders who understand equanimity and vibrancy are the ones who have figured out how to listen to their hearts in alignment with their heads.

They take time to be healthy—to have sufficient energy and a positive mindset. They exude confidence, but this is shared among their team. They know their worth, and it's not attached to the identity that they've achieved.

In this day and age, in-the-know leaders look at corporate wellness with a different view. Now, it's all about employee retention. How can we look after our employees to the best of our abilities, above and beyond an excellent salary, a benefits package, a bonus structure, etc.?

Ultimately, every human being—regardless of their title or stature—wants to be seen, heard, loved, and validated. Corporate wellness is all about the CEO sharing their vision so everyone in the company can be aligned. When we're united behind an idea as part of a team, corporate wellness is vital. It's shared happiness. It shows, as a company, that everyone can do amazing things. Corporate wellness is about highlighting our imperfections, allowing vulnerability to show and be present. After all, we're all imperfect.

Corporate wellness is also about taking your company brand and matching team behavior to it. It's not just about dialogue. It's accompanied by setting and following through on goals and actions to achieve company-wide synchronicity.

Corporate wellness talks about mindful leadership using words like "love" and "heart." But if you look at business acumen, words like love and compassion have never appeared. Why is that?

Corporate wellness is examining, assessing, and being holistic toward all things within a company. It is the foundation that drives the company to success, whether from a stance or monetary value standpoint.

Again, we must look at the whole picture and know that the foundation is the people. The foundation is the strong, healthy, vital culture that makes a company thrive. And when you can master the art of having a heart in your life, it shows up in your leadership too.

If you can handle a day-to-day situation and always convert it to include elements of being heart-centered, corporate wellness will grow healthy globally.

When we honor our connections with people without obligation, when we celebrate our relationships with people—everything stems from that. It allows us to dream, create, and adhere to daily behaviors of discipline and structure. Yet we can sit back, smile, and know we are joyful in this life journey. We know that our self-worth is not attached to identity—meaning all that we choose to participate in comes from a place of non-obligation. We are people, not job titles.

Energy is everything. It is us as our own person, and everything in and around the world. When energy is out of balance, so many things can occur. Just look at the world now; you'll see what I am talking about.

There is always time to pause. There is always time to breathe.

FULL-CIRCLE LIFE MOMENT:
When I closed my medical-case-management practice, I was empty. I was on emotional and physical overdraft in all areas of energy management. The learning moment for me was realizing self-care is not selfish. When I nourish myself daily, I am the best version of me for all aspects of my personal life and business.

♥

To help others develop,
start with yourself.

—MARSHALL GOLDSMITH

♥

CHAPTER 15

THE BEAUTY OF IMPERFECTION

———

How can embracing our imperfections and vulnerabilities help us become better leaders?

Eight weeks into the global pandemic, I sat at my desk thinking about my conversations with global leaders.

Two recurring themes continued to rumble through my mind:

1. What do I tell my people?
2. How do I navigate this pandemic?

Fear, apprehension, and uncertainty prevailed. Then, the lightbulb moment happened: *What if?*

What if you shared how you were feeling as the company's leader?

What if you told your people you didn't have the answer and were fearful?

What if you shared that you are imperfect?

At that moment, I knew I needed to talk about this and bring it to the world. That's how *Imperfect: The Heart-Centered Leadership Podcast* was born in May 2020.

Since then, I have had the honor and privilege of interviewing over 250 leaders from around the globe. We are now in season four!

When I ask the one question that has a permanent residency on the podcast, it prompts excellent conversation. It usually starts with a blank look from my guest leader, then instant laughter during an intentionally fun-spirited, spontaneous moment.

When the laughter stops, they ask, "Seriously, Deb, how much time do we have?"

This is because I have asked: What imperfections do you bring to your heart-centered leadership?

Leaders from all sectors are imperfect. I tell you this wholeheartedly, having interviewed so many. They can laugh at their imperfections because they are aligned with who they are. Their level of self-awareness is untouchable, and they are the first to laugh at themselves.

What I have learned is that we, as human beings, are also all imperfect.

The intriguing aspect is that not everyone feels at ease acknowledging or discussing their imperfections. My assessment of each leader was deliberate and calculated as I took on this project. I made sure to conduct thorough research and due diligence. It was my objective to include a diverse array of leaders from various sectors and regions around the world.

With technology, we are all connected and borderless. And being heart-centered and imperfect connects us all even further. What sector we work in is irrelevant—because we are all in the people business.

IMPERFECTION IN LEADERSHIP

Embracing imperfection as a leader can have its positives, such as:

- Making you more relatable and approachable to your team members, who may feel more comfortable sharing their own imperfections and struggles with you.
- Fostering a culture of honesty and openness, in which mistakes are viewed as opportunities for growth and learning.
- Helping you become more self-aware and humbler, leading to better decision-making and collaboration with your team.
- Inspiring your team to take risks and try new things, knowing mistakes are okay.
- And ultimately leading to more incredible innovation and creativity within your organization.

INTROVERT/EXTROVERT IMPERFECTION

Introverts may be more likely to internalize their feelings of imperfection, while extroverts may be more likely to seek validation and reassurance from others. However, it's important to remember that everyone is unique, and there is no one-size-fits-all approach to dealing with imperfection.

Being an introvert, I have never been focused on a perfect outcome for my podcast. Instead, I've wanted to embrace the process, develop good interview questions, behave my brand, and be heart-centered for each guest. To date, we are not on anyone's top-ten list—which is fine with me, as I love a certain amount of obscurity.

NAVIGATING IMPERFECTION IN BUSINESS ACUMEN

It's my goal to continue this critical conversation about imperfection. I see professionals with fantastic work experience and academic credentials daily and are unhappy with who they are and what they do daily.

Navigating imperfection in business requires accepting mistakes and finding ways to learn and improve. Establishing a culture of transparency, accountability, and continuous improvement is essential to minimize our imperfections' impact. This can be achieved through effective communication, regular feedback, and a willingness to adapt to changing circumstances. Focusing on solutions instead of blame can also help.

When we accept our imperfections, we live an entire, whole life. I aim to continue the conversation to show that imperfection has a place in business, in our leadership language.

The perfection fable teaches that striving for perfection can be a never-ending cycle leading to unhappiness and dissatisfaction. It encourages us to embrace our imperfections and find contentment in our efforts toward improvement.

Being imperfect is a choice and a wise way to simply live and be. Perfection, on the other hand, is an intangible reality we are taught as young children. I truly believe that seeking perfection is our gateway to stress and burnout. Bu thankfully, we have the choice to change the channel of thought and redirect ourselves.

IMPERFECTION IS BEAUTIFUL

The Japanese art of *kintsugi*, literally "to join with gold," dates to the fifteenth century and serves as a reminder to look on the bright side of things when they break.

FINDING PEACE WITH IMPERFECTION

Having inner peace means accepting ourselves as we are—flaws and all—and not striving for perfection. It means recognizing that those flaws are a natural part of being human and that they don't define our worth.

When we take the time to be quiet and reflect, imperfection is truly the foundation of our being. We all want to be happy and healthy during our lifetime—but life does not allow us to live or learn without mistakes.

Imperfection is listening to the whispers that come from within. There is no right way. Perhaps imperfect brilliance is the way.

How many times have you seen or heard something that is brand new and thought, how simple and brilliant is that?

I want to tell you that you are capable of amazing things. Excellence comes from trial and error. If we look at any invention, it wasn't developed on the first try. The same philosophy goes for being a heart-centered leader. Embrace your imperfections and *try.*

The best part is if you fail forward, you can get back up and keep going. I know this from my own life. I have developed many affirmations along the way and balance them with my imperfection.

These four strategies are part of my daily heart-centered leadership and align with my imperfection:

1. Making a difference in this busy, loud world is my superpower.
2. Staying self-directed in my thoughts is my strategy.
3. I will always be the reason someone will smile today.
4. Kindness is always in style.

FULL-CIRCLE LIFE MOMENT:
The values of heart-centered leadership I tried to use and lead with in my twenties were not accepted back then. I led with them and used them daily, and those who wanted to receive goodness did so. Those who chose not to receive gently slipped away. And to this day, I embrace my imperfection.

The global pandemic allowed me more time and space to be me.

I leaned in to:

♥ Ensure my self-belief remains limitless
♥ Encourage my voice to speak
♥ Deepen my level of listening to hear
♥ Speak my truth without fear
♥ Write with more heart
♥ Travel around the globe to virtually meet and interview over 250 heart-centered leaders
♥ Feel empowered by many women

Connection with people is the key to happiness and success, as it allows us to look inward and feel valued, heard, and validated.

♥

A leader takes people
where they want to go.

A great leader takes people
where they don't necessarily
want to go, but ought to be.

—ROSALYNN SMITH CARTER

♥

CHAPTER 16

THE INTEGRATION OF LIFE AND LEADERSHIP

———

How can we balance the demands of our home and work lives while still maintaining a heart-centered leadership approach?

It's clear that balancing your personal and professional life can help you become a more effective, compassionate, and fulfilled leader.

I remember my own mother, nicely dressed each day as if she worked in an office. Her work-life balance skills were exercised like those of a facility manager. She excelled in all the logistics of running a home, including knowing her place. Back then, this was standard. But, as decades passed, working women who were also wives and mothers embraced work-life balance as the combination of Betty Crocker, June Cleaver, and Martha Stewart. Now *that* is an excellent work-life balance skillset.

Working women range from fantastic stay-at-home moms to CEOs of large companies. Their commonality is that they share the same goals, just on different levels. It's a daily struggle for many; however, they all have well-honed talents of pure and simple acceptance and the ability to juggle and prioritize.

Who was our role model for work-life balance?

This is something to think about.

Do we need to conform to a role model?

Is there a perfect person on Earth who can do it all?

Sure, maybe it can be done with a massive support system in place. But there isn't a standalone system that encompasses basic decision-making logistics and the mastered skill of delegation.

Self-inflicted stress is not going to lead you to work-life balance. A recent Harvard study found that women are extremely hard on themselves, trying to be that perfect mom or wife whose value system their behavior is modeled on (Beard 2020).

I spent much time alone as a child, which led me to want to be noticed by anyone. This is how overachievers are born. We want anyone to see, compliment, and, of course, *like* us. But as I reached midlife, overachieving no longer served me—in fact, it burned me out. I was there to help anyone, any time, do anything. Now, I've hung up my Superwoman cape and poured everything back into myself.

Having your life in balance is a good thing. Saying no does not make you a wrong person. Rather, it fights off the stress ninjas in your life and sets healthy boundaries you can live within. Make a promise to yourself to be good to you, *for* you. Throw perfection to the curb. Progression in life is not about perfection; it's about doing what is good for you, always.

When you can let go of people and things that no longer serve you, your life opens to unlimited possibilities. You decide what you want to do and when. You decide who is part of your inner tribe, based only on feeling good about people who want nothing from you but your company.

As you move forward, allow yourself to withdraw from all the emotional debt in your life.

Work-life balance: three simple words. Yet many people struggle to understand the meaning of this achievable life.

What if I asked you to replace the word "balance" with "integration"?

Does it offer you ease?

Work-life balance is not a trend. It's a decision coupled with time management skills, ultimately leading to a lifestyle of meaning in your career and personal life. Life is not meant to be lived with perfectly outlined daily schedules. Emergencies happen, life happens. The key is to decide how to respond to these bumps along life's highways, then, more importantly, get back on track.

Society has put us on a fast track for everything, with busy schedules at work and home. This is so prevalent that activities surround our children before and after school. It's no wonder drive-thru restaurants were created. Again, no set equation exists to determine how to live with a work-life balance. It boils down to one element: acceptance. Your lifestyle dictates how your personal and work lives will ebb and flow.

Is there an actual science to happiness? Well, people who have a good balance between work and life—and can keep it up—seem happy and satisfied.

SETTING BOUNDARIES

Setting boundaries is essential for maintaining healthy relationships and avoiding burnout in both personal and professional contexts.

Here are some practical tips for setting boundaries in life and leadership.

- Know your values and priorities: Identify what you want to work on personally and professionally, then use that as a guide to set boundaries that align with your vision.
- Communicate clearly and assertively: Be clear about your needs and expectations and convey them in a direct and respectful manner. Use "I" statements and avoid blaming or criticizing others.
- Learn to say no: Saying no is an essential part of setting boundaries. Be firm but polite and offer alternative solutions if possible.

- Set realistic expectations: Avoid overcommitting or taking on more than you can handle. Only take on realistic goals and deadlines, and delegate tasks when necessary.
- Take care of yourself: Prioritize self-care activities, such as exercise, meditation, and time with loved ones. This will help you recharge and maintain healthy integration.

Remember, setting boundaries takes practice and may require some trial and error. Don't be afraid to adjust your boundaries as needed to ensure they are working for you and your team.

TIME MANAGEMENT

We all have the same amount of time each week, 168 hours, to fit everything into our schedule—and overseeing how we spend our months, weeks, minutes, and seconds can be a tumultuous task.

What does your weekly schedule breakdown look like?

Task	Time Spent	Scenario/Variance
Work	40 hours	Based on a full-time job
Sleep	56 hours	Based on 8 hours per night
Exercise	7 hours	1 hour, 7 days per week
Social	8 hours	Date Night 4 hours, Networking 4 hours
Self-Care	7 hours	60 minutes per day
Family	35 hours	Based on 5 hours/day
Friends	3 hours	Based on 1 or 2 visits
Spiritual/Faith	1.5 hours	Based on a service/meditation
TOTAL	157.5 hours	Does this look like your weekly work-life balance equation?

You will note from the above table that there are 157.5 hours based on its hypothetical example of work, sleep, exercise, social life, self-care, family, friends, and spiritual time.

What would you do with the remaining ten and a half hours in your week?

Managing time takes patience, practice, and constant assessment to achieve what's best for you and your family. Your schedule and task list will constantly change; however, if you have a plan, you are setting a foundation for success.

Each element can change from week to week. A perfect example is work: Given the landscape of today's working conditions, you may be an in-office, remote, or hybrid worker. You may also have overtime, take holidays, or enjoy a statutory holiday. All of which makes your schedule unique to you.

CHALLENGES TO WORK-LIFE INTEGRATION AND HOW TO MANAGE THEM

Traveling for work can be a factor that tips the scales toward imbalance. In this case, you need to find the ten-minute time "zappers" and eliminate them. It's equally important to follow a traveling routine and not let technology's beeps and alarms become a work-life balance bomb that constantly interrupts you and challenges your attention and concentration.

Why do we strive for perfection? What *is* perfection? Is it a generationally reoccurring belief system? When does life become "happy" for people? Does work-life balance bring happiness and success? Is there a genetic predisposition? Is it in our DNA? Do we repeat what our parents did? Or do we strive to do and be better? Is work-life balance based on materialism? And is this what we base our successes on in life?

Work-life integration is about growth, acceptance, and progression—not perfection. Think about it like riding a bike. It's all about repetition and your attitude, about falling off and then getting back on. How can you grow without losses and lessons? This is what you can foster and sustain: well-honed core beliefs and a mastery of work-life balance.

Work-life balance develops as you age, then matures as you experience lifestyle changes and achieve your goals and dreams. It's an ongoing reevaluation of who you are and what you want from the different parts of your life.

Many people get stuck and do not know where to start. Milestones turn into tremendous accomplishments. Milestones help you track your journey, while accomplishments highlight your successes and contributions along the way. Finish tasks and projects, set a goal to do one big thing per day, and do not waiver.

In the end, work-life integration comes down to communication and acceptance.

Communication is a critical factor for balanced integration—both with your family for your personal life and with your employer and clients for your work life. Each aspect can be in sync if the lines of communication flow smoothly. And such synchronization demonstrates that you've intentionally placed and designed your life.

Accept change—because life *will* happen. Work-life integration can be one's acceptance of what is. For example, you are swamped at work, your house is messy, and your child is sick. All of this can throw a curveball and disrupt anyone's balance. The point is to accept the imbalances and work out what is essential. Schedules, deadlines, and commitments will always be there—but sometimes, they must take a backseat.

Achieving a work-life integration is directly linked to a person's happiness. Many people suffer from depression related to their home or work lives or, unfortunately, both; this can be even more difficult without a support system. You must believe in yourself and know that more extraordinary things will always come into your life.

Here's a list of strategies to implement more balance in your life.

1. Schedule the important things
2. Exercise time management
3. Communicate with your employer about flex time
4. Bring in a back-up
5. Communicate with other families
6. Be mindful of scheduling too many extracurriculars
7. Schedule routine, regular family time
8. Take time for yourself
9. Ensure you have coupled time
10. Share your work experience with your children
11. Make time for fun
12. Don't miss those special moments

CREATING A SUPPORTIVE AND INCLUSIVE WORK ENVIRONMENT

Having a caring, equitable external environment is essential for fostering collaboration, creativity, and productivity among team members. Here are some strategies for building a supportive and inclusive work environment.

- Foster open communication: Encourage team members to share their thoughts and ideas and create opportunities for feedback and discussion.
- Lead by example: Set the tone for inclusivity and respect by modeling inclusive behavior and language. Be aware of your own biases and work to overcome them.
- Create opportunities for growth and development: Offer professional development opportunities and training programs to help team members enhance their skills and advance their careers.
- Celebrate diversity: Recognize and appreciate all team members' unique perspectives and backgrounds. Celebrate cultural and religious holidays and events and incorporate diverse perspectives into decision-making.
- Address conflict promptly: Deal with conflicts or misunderstandings in a timely and respectful manner to avoid resentment and negativity.
- Provide support: Offer resources for mental health and well-being, such as an employee assistance program or access to a counselor.

Remember, building a supportive and inclusive work environment is an ongoing process that requires commitment and effort. By implementing these strategies, you can create a workplace culture that values diversity, promotes collaboration, and inspires excellence.

FULL-CIRCLE LIFE MOMENT:

At times I've been a professional with no work-life integration, leaving me empty on all levels. Instead, we can create and achieve our dreams with harmony, exchanging balance for integration.

♥

When we really connect to that place of
wisdom and strength and understanding,
everything becomes easier.

—ARIANNA HUFFINGTON

♥

CHAPTER 17

MY HEART-CENTERED LEADERSHIP JOURNEY

As I reflect upon my leadership journey and all its transformative experiences, I am filled with gratitude for the profound impact it has had on both my personal growth and the lives of those I've had the privilege to lead.

Embracing the principles of heart-centered leadership has allowed me to develop a deep connection with my authentic self and foster a culture of trust, compassion, and empowerment within the teams and organizations I've worked with globally.

Throughout this journey, I have understood that leadership is not simply about achieving targets or driving profits—but about creating a nurturing and inclusive environment where individuals can flourish and reach their full potential.

By cultivating a leadership style rooted in empathy, kindness, and integrity, I have witnessed the remarkable power in inspiring others to bring their best selves to their lives and leadership.

One of my most profound lessons-learned is that leadership begins with self-awareness and self-care. Nurturing my well-being and practicing self-compassion have allowed me to lead from a place of strength, resilience, and authenticity.

By prioritizing personal growth and development, I have been able to model the behavior and values I aspire to see in leaders and teams at all levels to truly foster a culture of personal and professional growth.

I realized that effective leadership is a continuous learning journey. It involves actively seeking feedback, embracing diversity of thought, and being open to new perspectives. By creating a safe space for dialogue and collaboration, I harnessed the collective intelligence of my clients, leading to innovative solutions and breakthrough moments.

Heart-centered leadership's deepest impact lies in the relationships built along the way. By recognizing and valuing each team member's unique strengths and contributions, I have forged deep connections with clients based on trust, respect, and genuine care. These bonds have created a harmonious working relationship and fostered a sense of belonging and fulfillment among team members.

As I conclude the final chapter of this playbook, I see that leadership is a force for positive change. Through the consistent practice of heart-centered leadership, we can create organizations and leaders that prioritize the well-being of all stakeholders, contribute to the betterment of society, and leave a legacy of inspiration and compassion.

May this heart-centered leadership playbook guide all leaders—present and future—to ignite a collective commitment to lead with purpose, authenticity, and love.

Let us nurture our hearts, empower those around us, and strive for a world where leadership is synonymous with empathy, understanding, and a deep respect for the inherent dignity of every individual.

Together, we can work toward a future in which leadership transforms lives and creates a more compassionate world.

RECOMMENDED READING

Alter, Cara Hale. *The Credibility Code*. Meritus Books, 2012.

Berkun, Scott. *The Myths of Innovation*. O'Reilly Media, Inc., 2010.

Boyd, Drew, and Jacob Goldenberg. *Inside the Box*. New York: Simon & Schuster, 2013.

Brown, Brené. *Atlas of the Heart*. Random House Books. 2021.

Brown, Brené. *The Gifts of Imperfection*. Center City: Hazelden Publishing, 2010.

Caesar, Vance, and Carol Ann Caesar. *The High Achiever's Guide to Happiness*. 2005.

Cadigan, Steve. *Workquake: Embracing the Aftershocks of COVID-19 to Create a Better Model of Working*. Amplify, 2021.

Cialdini, Robert B. *Influence: The Art of Persuasion*. New York: Harper Collins, 1984.

Coelho, Paulo. *The Alchemist*. New York: Harper One, 2005.

Covey, Stephen. *The 7 Habits of Highly Effective People*. New York: Simon & Schuster, 1989.

Edmondson, Amy. *The Fearless Organization: Creating Psychological Safety in the Workplace for Learning, Innovation, and Growth*. Wiley, 2018.

Ferrazzi, Keith. *Never Eat Alone*. New York: Crown Publishing, 2005.

Fournier, Camille, *The Manager's Path: A Guide for Tech Leaders Navigating Growth and Change*. O'Reilly Media, 2017.

Frankl, Viktor. *Man's Search for Meaning.* Boston: Beacon Press, 1946.

Gordon, Jon. *The Power of Positive Leadership: How and Why Positive Leaders Transform Teams and Organizations and Change the World.* Wiley, 2017.

Grant, Adam. *Give and Take.* New York: Penguin Books, 2014.

Hartman, Taylor. *The People Code.* New York: Scribner, 1987.

Hendricks, Gay. *The Big Leap.* New York: Harper Collins, 2010.

Kirkman, Bradley L., and Stoverink, Adam. *Unbreakable: Building and Leading Resilient Teams.* Stanford Business Books, 2023.

Krysa, Danielle. *Your Inner Critic is a Big Jerk.* San Francisco: Chronicle Books, 2016.

Lencioni, Patrick. *Overcoming the Five Dysfunctions of a Team: A Field Guide for Leaders, Managers, and Facilitators.* Jossey-Bass, 2005.

Macleod, Hugh. *Humanizing Leadership: Reflection Fuels, People Matter, Relationships Make The Difference.* FriesenPress, 2019.

Murthy, Vivek H. *Together: The Healing Power of Human Connection in a Sometimes Lonely World.* New York: Harper Collins, 2020.

Phillips, J.B. *Your God Is Too Small.* New York: Touchstone, 1997.

Sinek, Simon. *Start with Why.* New York: Penguin Random House, 2009.

Steinbrecher, Susan, and Bennett, Joel. *Heart-Centered Leadership: Lead Well, Live Well.* 3rd Edition. 2022.

RESOURCES

HEART-CENTERED LEADERSHIP BILL OF RIGHTS

You have the right to never feel bad about saying no (or yes) to other people.

❤

You have the right to deviate from one's intended path or to alter one's mind.

❤

You have the right to obtain your desired outcomes through discussion and compromise.

❤

You have the right to say all that you are feeling.

❤

You have the right to share your thoughts even if they're not shared by others.

❤

You have the right to be treated with kindness, thoughtfulness, and respect.

❤

You have the right to choose the people who are allowed to share your life.

❤

You have the right to share your limits and non-negotiables.

❤

You have the right to put yourself first without guilt.

❤

You have the right to be yourself, let your true self shine through, and enjoy your life.

❤

Crowe, Deborah. 2022. The Heart-Centered Leadership Bill of Rights.
Ontario, CA: Deb Crowe.

❤ HEART-CENTERED LEADERSHIP AFFIRMATION ❤

I have the ability to lead and inspire others.

My leadership qualities are evident to everyone around me. Over the years, I have developed the ability to lead a wide variety of people in any circumstance.

I have a level of natural charisma that people find irresistible. That makes it easy for people to trust and believe in my words and my vision. People are attracted to me and what I have to say. I am a person that people follow willingly.

It is my ability to inspire others that sets me apart.

I know how to motivate people and present a possible future that others find attractive. **When I inspire others, they can give me their best each day.** When I inspire others to do their best, I am demonstrating the depth of my leadership skills.

I am always perfecting my ability to lead and inspire. Though I already know so much, there is always more I can learn. I avoid becoming lazy and complacent. I am continuously improving my skills.

Leadership skills are at a premium in today's world. I know that my skills are valued throughout the world.

As my ability to lead grows, the number of opportunities available to me grows as well.

Today, I am taking full advantage of any opportunities to lead and inspire others. I am doing my best to be a great leader as I work on strengthening my leadership skills even further.

Self-Reflection Questions:

1. What opportunities do I have to be a leader in my life?
2. What can I do to enhance my leadership abilities?
3. What are my greatest strengths as a leader?

Crowe, Deborah. 2021. The Heart-Centered Leadership Affirmation.
Ontario, CA: Deb Crowe.

Crowe, Deborah. 2020. Heart-Centered Leadership Qualities. Ontario, CA: Deb Crowe.

This document has traveled around the
world and is now available in
twenty-five languages.
You can download here:

ACKNOWLEDGMENTS

This book has been a labor of love.

A special message of love and gratitude to my husband John, my true BFF, my rock, my confidante, my love. To our two beautiful daughters, Christine and Laura, our heart-centered leaders who are well on their way in life and leadership. I love you all for being the best family and for your deep love and support for everything I do.

To my granddaughter Eleanor, this book is for you! Our future leader!

To every leader who has taught me along the way in my life, I have learned from every single one of you.

Every experience I have had in life and leadership is a true gift and a welcomed addition to my personal and professional development, creating a toolkit that keeps growing and evolving daily.

To my Author Community, I am so grateful for your support, excitement and following me on this journey. I am so proud to list all of you in my book:

Josie Blake, Nadine Khemlall, Cynthia Brunditt, Lovedeep Singh, Jennifer Noel, Melissa Carson, Michael Bee, Lisa Schwerzmann, Tina Bakehouse, Nicholas D'Souza, Stephanie Piper, Rob Greenly, Robert Labrecque, Rada Medic, Mike Greenly, Tania Demelo, Jean-Marie Fiala, Vijay Chandler, John Hilbrich, Brenda Bourns, Christine Snider, Angela Zehr, Steven Lipton, Rod Anderson, Markus Neukom, Catherine McIntosh, Scott Quinney, Melanie Gardin, Melissa Dodge, Kathy Collett, Eric Koester, Robert and Therese Kuenzlen, Kerri Whitehead, Laura Crowe, Steve and Mary MacClure, Gary Danner, Heather Carey, Fanshawe College (School of Access Studies), Paula Morand, Jo-Anne Martin, Kelly Towers, Dr. Paul Woods, Jennifer Lacy, Dana Sciuto, Jenny Betancourt, Adrienne Sanders, Marie Reig Florensa.

I look forward to visiting the organizations that requested Heart-Centered Leadership Fireside Chats. It will be an honor to sit with you and your staff and sign twenty-five copies of my book!

To my local supporters, I welcome the opportunity to meet all of you and sign your book personally!

For my supporters far and wide, I will sign your book and send it with as much love and excitement to you!

To Professor Eric Koester for his vision to help authors write their stories and the incredible team at Manuscripts LLC, your unwavering support will always have a special place in my heart.

To Irene Kavanagh for helping me with my edits as I navigated some hard times in my own life during this editing process.

To all my beta readers: your honesty, transparency, and the gift of your time will always be an heirloom memory engraved in my heart.

To my mentor Steve MacClure, I know you look down on me and smile. You always believed in me and gently encouraged me to start my company in 1990.

A special thank you to Scott Aronowitz, my developmental editor; Pavita Singh, my structural editor; Whitney McGruder, my revisions editor; and Jacques Moolman for helping me craft my message and getting me to the finish line of publishing! Writing this playbook has been one of the most incredible experiences of my life.

APPENDIX

—

CHAPTER 2: KINDNESS IS THE WAY

Women of Influence. 2023. "The Tallest Poppy." Women of Influence. Accessed on May 29, 2023.
https://www.womenofinfluence.ca/tps/.

CHAPTER 3: THE HEART-CENTERED LEADERSHIP BILL OF RIGHTS

Crowe, Deborah. 2022. *The Heart-Centered Leadership Bill of Rights.* Ontario, CA: Deb Crowe.

CHAPTER 4: THE HEART-CENTERED LEADERSHIP AFFIRMATION

Crowe, Deborah. 2021. *The Heart-Centered Leadership Affirmation.* Ontario, CA: Deb Crowe.

CHAPTER 5: MIDLIFE WISDOM—EMBRACE BEING A MODERN ELDER

Crowe, Deb. 2022. "Episode 194: Embracing the Modern Elder with Chip Conley." *imperfect: The Heart-Centered Leadership Podcast.* May 25, 2022. 34 min. https://podcasts.apple.com/ca/podcast/episode-194-embracing-the-modern-elder-with-chip-conley/id1518475768?i=1000563850035.

Locker, Melissa. 2018. "Airbnb's Chip Conley Is Doubling Down on Being a 'Modern Elder.'" *Fast Company* (blog). October 23, 2018. https://www.fastcompany.com/90255475/airbnbs-chip-conley-is-doubling-down-on-being-a-modern-elder.

Netzley, Michael. 2021. "A Brain-Energy Platform: Bringing Verifiable Vibrancy to a Billion Careers." Extend My Runway Pte Ltd. January 1, 2022. https://drive.google.com/file/d/1b2B3EdYXLiIu4YQFbeJzXBkOh3xo9tpK/view.

CHAPTER 6: LEADERSHIP IN THE WAKE OF TRAGEDY
Rashid, Marghalara, Helly R. Goez, Neelam Mabood, Samah Damanhoury, Jerome Y. Yager, Anthony S. Joyce, Amanda S. Newton. 2014. "The Impact of Pediatric Traumatic Brain Injury (TBI) on Family Functioning: A Systematic Review." *J Pediatr Rehabil Med* 7, no. 3: 241–54. DOI: 10.3233/PRM-140293.

CHAPTER 8: HEART-CENTERED LEADERSHIP QUALITIES
Crowe, Deborah. 2020. *Heart-Centered Leadership Qualities*. Ontario, CA: Deb Crowe.

CHAPTER 9: THE HEART-CENTERED LEADERSHIP MODEL
Bourke, Juliet. 2016. "The Six Signature Traits of Inclusive Leadership." *Deloitte Insights* (blog). April 14, 2016. https://www2.deloitte.com/us/en/insights/topics/talent/six-signature-traits-of-inclusive-leadership.html.

Crowe, Deborah. 2021. *The Heart-Centered Leadership Model*. Ontario, CA: Deb Crowe.

David, Susan. 2022. "Emotional Pyramid of Needs." *Susan David* (blog). October 12, 2022. https://www.susandavid.com/resource/emotional-pyramid-of-needs.

Maslow, Abraham H. 1943. "A Theory of Human Motivation." *Psychological Review* 50, no. 4: 370–396. https://doi.org/10.1037/h0054346.

CHAPTER 10: BUSINESS ACUMEN WITH HEART
La Monica, Paul R. 2022. "Mike Sievert of T-Mobile is the CNN Business CEO of the Year." CNN Business (blog). December 26, 2022. https://www.cnn.com/2022/12/26/investing/ceo-of-the-year-tmobile-mike-sievert.

Sievert, Mike. 2021. "Leading by Learning." T-Mobile USA, Inc. (blog). April 16, 2021. https://www.t-mobile.com/news/community/ceo-mike-sievert-growth-mindset-leadership-lessons.

Sievert, Mike. 2022. "My 10th Magentaversary: Reflecting on a Decade of Work Alongside the Best in Wireless." T-Mobile USA, Inc. (blog). November 22, 2022. https://www.t-mobile.com/news/un-carrier/ceo-mike-sievert-10-year-work-magentaversary.

CHAPTER 11: THE SELF-CARE JOURNEY IN LEADERSHIP
Klug, Katharina, Jörg Felfe, and Annika Krick. 2022. "Does Self-Care Make You a Better Leader? A Multisource Study Linking Leader Self-Care to Health-Oriented

Leadership, Employee Self-Care, and Health." *Int J Environ Res Public Health* 19, no. 11 (May): 6733. DOI: 10.3390/ijerph19116733.

Martínez, Nicole, Cynthia D. Connelly, Alexa Pérez, and Patricia Calero. 2021. "Self-Care: A Concept Analysis." *International Journal of Nursing Sciences* 8, no. 4 (Oct): 418–425. DOI: 10.1016/j.ijnss.2021.08.007.

CHAPTER 12: FORGIVENESS IN LEADERSHIP

The University of Texas Permian Basin. 2023. "How Much of Communication Is Nonverbal?" The University of Texas Permian Basin (blog). Accessed on April 24, 2023. https://online.utpb.edu/about-us/articles/communication/how-much-of-communication-is-nonverbal/.

CHAPTER 13: THE VALUE OF INTUITION MANAGEMENT

Adams, Gerard. 2020. "How to Unlock the Full Power of Your Intuition." *Entrepreneur* (blog). June 23, 2020. https://www.entrepreneur.com/leadership/how-to-unlock-the-full-power-of-your-intuition/352256.

Ferenstein, Gregory. 2016. "Netflix CEO Explains Why 'Gut' Decisions Still Rule in The Era of Big Data." *Forbes* (blog). January 22, 2016. https://www.forbes.com/sites/gregoryferenstein/2016/01/22/netflix-ceo-explains-why-gut-decisions-still-rule-in-the-era-of-big-data/?sh=636771451e09.

CHAPTER 14: MANAGING THE INNER LEADER

Almekinder, Elisabeth. 2021. "Forest or Nature Bathing: Ancient Practices, Modern Uses, and the Science of Relaxation." Blue Zones (blog). April 28, 2021. https://www.bluezones.com/2019/06/forest-or-nature-bathing-ancient-practices-modern-uses-and-the-science-of-relaxation/.

Brach, Tara. 2023. "Feeling Overwhelmed? Try the RAIN Meditation." *Mindful* (blog). February 17, 2023. https://www.mindful.org/tara-brach-rain-mindfulness-practice/.

Bunch, Erin. 2021. "Navy SEALs Use a Technique Called 'Box Breathing' To Relieve Stress and So Can You." *Well + Good* (blog). April 4, 2021. https://www.wellandgood.com/box-breathing/.

Jeraci, Allison Ray. 2023. "What Is Yoga Nidra & Its Benefits." Yoga International (blog). Accessed on May 29, 2023. https://yogainternational.com/article/view/5-benefits-of-yoga-nidra/.

Loehr, Jim and Tony Schwartz. 2004. *The Power of Full Engagement*. New York: Simon & Schuster. https://www.simonandschuster.com/books/The-Power-of-Full-Engagement/Jim-Loehr/9780743226752.

Karode, Sandeep. 2020. "A Brief History of Physics of Pranayama." Medium (blog). April 22, 2020. https://sandeepkarode.medium.com/a-brief-history-of-physics-of-pranayama-6793d15dbc79.

Soulful Soundwaves. 2023. "The Science Behind Our Music." Soulful Soundwaves (blog). Accessed on June 18, 2023. https://www.soulfulsoundwaves.com/the-science.

Wellons, Alyce E. 2023. "Starting Your Day with Sankalpa, the Power of Intention." Kripalu Center for Yoga & Health (blog). Accessed on May 29, 2023. https://kripalu.org/resources/starting-your-day-sankalpa-power-intention.

CHAPTER 16: THE INTEGRATION OF LIFE AND LEADERSHIP

Beard, Alison. 2020. "Ideal Worker or Perfect Mom?" Harvard Business Review (blog). January 10, 2020. https://hbr.org/2019/01/ideal-worker-or-perfect-mom?registration=success.

Printed in Great Britain
by Amazon

30109112R00137